Guita⌐

C000157197

and Gear

Everything you need to know in an
easy-to-follow format!

John Carruthers
Tobias Hurwitz

Alfred Music
P.O. Box 10003
Van Nuys, CA 91410-0003
alfred.com

Copyright © MMXIV by Alfred Music
All rights reserved. Printed in USA.

Library of Congress Control Number: 2013955800

ISBN-10: 0-7390-9636-2
ISBN-13: 978-0-7390-9636-9

Photos courtesy of Larry Lytle
Rocktron HUSH pedal courtesy of Rocktron

 Alfred Cares. Contents printed on environmentally responsible paper.

Contents

About the Authors

John Carruthers started repairing and building guitars nearly 40 years ago in a converted garage in West Los Angeles. Over the years, John has built a reputation among players and manufacturers for his knowledge and quality workmanship. John was a staff writer for *Guitar Player* magazine for nearly 10 years, authoring the Guitar Workshop column and writing product reviews.

John's many inventions include products and techniques like the multi-saddle compensated bridge for acoustic guitars and basses used by such companies as Takamine, Lowden, and Guild. Another of his innovations is a stereo pickup system for acoustic guitars using a microphone and piezo transducer or magnetic soundhole pickup. He designed and built the neck-duplicating machine currently used by the Fender custom shop.

John has done consulting and prototype work for many manufacturers including Fender, Music Man, Yamaha, Ibanez, G&L, and EMG. Some of his more notable projects include working with artists on their signature models. John has worked with such noted players as Joe Pass, Lee Ritenour, Robben Ford, Eric Clapton, Eddie Van Halen, Steve Vai, and many more.

Carruthers Guitars currently occupies a modern, 5000 square foot repair and manufacturing facility in Venice, California and continues to repair and build high-quality instruments under John's leadership.

GIT graduate **Tobias Hurwitz** resides in Baltimore, Maryland where he has been avidly playing guitar since 1977. In the summertime, Tobias directs the Rock Star Jam music camp in Baltimore and teaches at the Crown of the Continent Guitar Festival in Montana and the Ruby Mountain Guitar Summit in West Virginia. Tobias has written 15 guitar books on a wide range of topics, from rock guitar and note-for-note transcriptions to zen guitar and how to get the best tones from your gear. He is widely published by major guitar magazines such as *Guitar Player* and was prominently featured in the best-selling book *Guitar Zero* by Gary Marcus. Tobias holds the patent and trademark to his innovative invention, The Shred-o-Meter, which is the world's first musical note speedometer, measuring the notes per second (NPS) that a guitarist can play. Visit www.tobiashurwitz.com to sign up for guitar lessons via Skype!

Introduction

Most guitarists are unfamiliar with adjusting or maintaining their guitar. This is unfortunate because proper adjustment and maintenance of their instrument will enhance the sound and playability while prolonging its life. Even the simplest task, such as changing the strings properly, can pose great difficulty to someone who has not been shown the proper method. In this book, we will show you the best ways to string, polish, and adjust your instrument, as well as learn about, maintain and, in some cases, utilize your gear in different ways.

Note: *Though this book is mostly concerned with the electric guitar and its corresponding gear, you will find occasional notes or references to the acoustic guitar.*

PART 1: GUITAR CARE

Electric Guitar

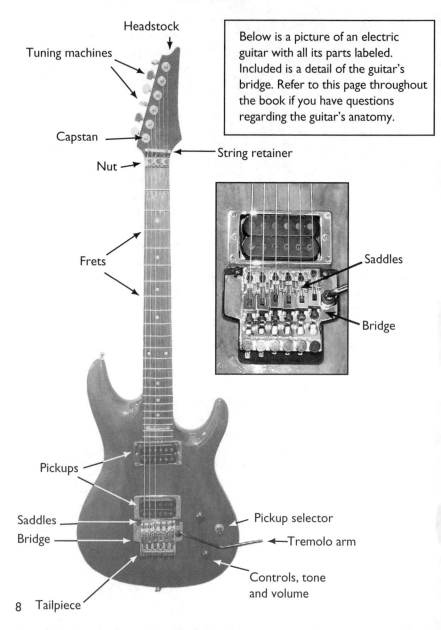

Below is a picture of an electric guitar with all its parts labeled. Included is a detail of the guitar's bridge. Refer to this page throughout the book if you have questions regarding the guitar's anatomy.

Headstock

Tuning machines

Capstan

Nut

String retainer

Frets

Saddles

Bridge

Pickups

Saddles

Bridge

Pickup selector

Tremolo arm

Controls, tone and volume

8 Tailpiece

GENERAL SETUP
Changing the Strings

Before attempting to set up your guitar, it is very important to install new strings. As strings get old, they become corroded, filled with oils and perspiration, and dented by the frets. This will cause the string to vibrate in an erratic manner and interfere with proper intonation and action adjustment.

Removing Old Strings

First, remove the old strings from your guitar. The best way to do this will vary with the type of bridge assembly you have.

For guitars with locking tremolos, you should start with Step 1. With other guitars, proceed to Step 3.

Step 1: Release the locking nut.

Step 2: Insert a spacer (see photo below) between the rear edge of the bridge and the top of the guitar. This will stabilize the floating motion and make re-tuning much easier. You can use a piece of wooden doweling or cork.

Spacer

Step 3: De-tune the strings until slack. Release the string locks on the bridge saddles and remove the strings. Be careful not to misplace any loose parts, floating bridges, nuts, or other hardware.

After the strings have been removed is a perfect opportunity to clean and polish your guitar (see pages 68–81).

Installing New Strings

The proper installation of strings is very important! It will help eliminate the number one source of tuning problems and string breakage: poorly installed strings.

Most electric guitars with conventional tuning machines can be strung the same way:

Step 1: Insert the string through the appropriate hole in the tailpiece, guide it over the saddle and nut, then insert it through the hole in the capstan.

Step 2: With your left hand maintaining tension on the string past the tuning gear, and your right hand grasping the string midway down the neck, create enough slack above the fingerboard (approximately 3" or 76.2 mm, see note below) to allow sufficient winds on the capstan. As you lift the string at the midpoint of the fingerboard, use your index finger to gauge the proper distance (see photo on the following page). This should allow approximately two-to-three turns around the capstan.

This will ensure a strong hold on the string while reducing the chance of breakage due to a concentration of stress.

NOTE

mm = millimeters. A measurement from the metric system equaling one thousandth of a meter. A meter is equal to 39.37".

" = inch or inches.

Using your index finger to gauge proper amount of slack.

Step 3: "Lock" the string by bringing the loose end over the capstan toward the center of the headstock and looping it under the captured string between the nut and the capstan.

Step 4: Next, bend the string up and back toward the middle of the neck.

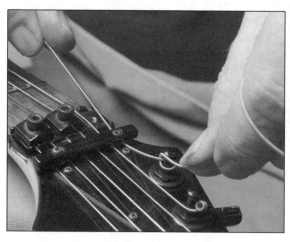

Step 5: While maintaining tension on the string with your right hand, wind the string in a downward spiral onto the capstan. Once the string comes to tension, you may release your right hand.

Step 6: Using wire cutters, cut off the excess string.

Locking Tuners

There are two types of locking tuners: manual and auto. Manual tuners require the player to insert the string in the capstan hole, take up the slack, and then manually lock the knob on the back of the tuner. Auto lockers require no action on the part of the player—just insert the string through the capstan, take up the slack and tune to pitch. (Guitars equipped with locking tremolo systems require a different procedure—see page 108.)

Manual locking tuner.

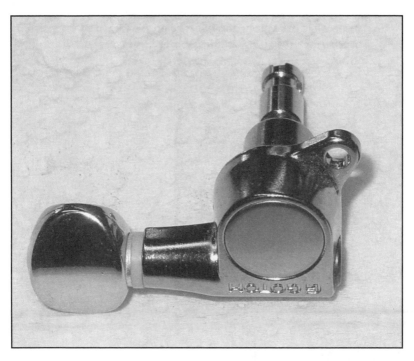

Auto locking tuner.

Stretching the Strings

Stretching the strings will help them stay in tune. If you have a Floyd Rose system, before locking the nut, it is advisable to adjust your fine tuners to nearly the full out position before stretching your strings.

Step 1: Grasp the string between the thumb and the first finger of the picking hand.

Step 2: Raise the string *slightly* above the fingerboard, sliding your fingers and thumb along the length of the string while maintaining this outward position. Don't over-stretch the string, as it might break.

Step 3: Retune and repeat this procedure until the tuning stabilizes.

Step 4: Finally, if you have a Floyd Rose, lock the nut clamps with an Allen wrench.

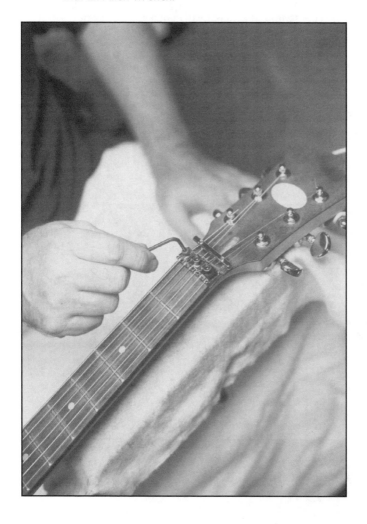

Stringing Fender Slotted Machine Heads

Some Fender guitars and basses have tuning machines with a slotted capstan. This style of machine head requires a different method of stringing.

It is necessary to allow slightly more slack than with normal tuning machines (approximately 5" or 12.5 cm).

Step 1: Bend the end of the string 90 degrees and cut to length.

Step 2: Insert the bent end into the capstan as shown in the photograph below.

Step 3: While maintaining tension on the string with your right hand, wind the string in a downward spiral onto the capstan.

On basses, the procedure is the same except you must leave more slack due to the increased diameter of the capstan and strings. The bass strings should extend approximately 8" or about 18 cm. past the capstan.

NOTE

In both cases, it is advisable to bend the string before cutting. This prevents the outer wraps from slipping and the string from going dead.

Truss Rod Adjustment

The first step in setting up a guitar should be the truss rod adjustment. Before getting started, the guitar should be strung with the brand and gauge of strings you prefer and tuned to pitch. Depending on how your guitar is made, you will need an Allen wrench, a screwdriver, or a socket driver.

The truss rod adjustment changes the *bow* (curve; see illustration on next page) of the neck and affects all other adjustments, including action and intonation. A nut for adjusting the truss rod appears at the head or at the heel of the guitar.

Contrary to popular belief, guitar necks must have a certain amount of inward bow to play properly. Strings vibrate in slow curves with the largest curve being at their midpoint. Having a small amount of bow in the neck accommodates this motion. Too much bow has a sharping affect on the strings, since it increases the distance a string must stretch to reach the fret. It makes playing more difficult for the same reason. A reverse bow (outward) causes the strings to buzz against the frets in the lower registers (closer to the nut).

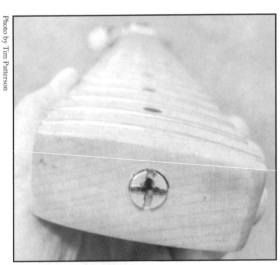

Photo by Tim Patterson

Truss rod, front view.

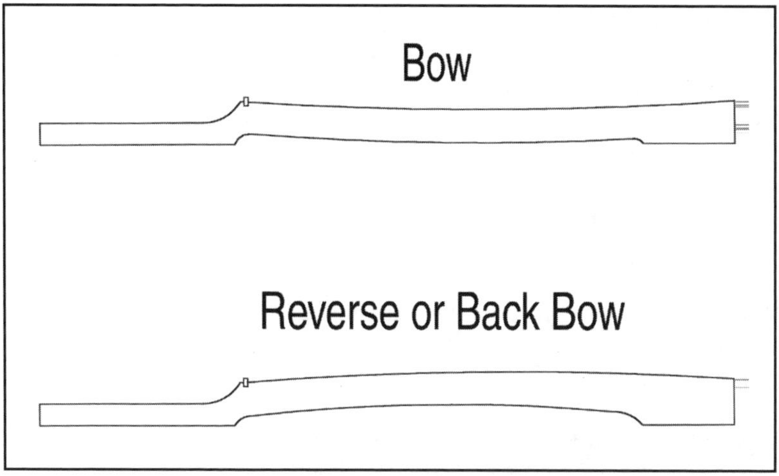

Bow

Reverse or Back Bow

NOTE

All guitar necks must have a little bow. In the illustration above, the bow is exaggerated for the purpose of demonstration.

Direction of Adjustment

With most truss rods, bow is reduced by turning the adjustment-nut clockwise, strengthening the neck. Counterclockwise movement causes a relaxation in the neck, increasing the natural bow created by string tension. You should always face the screw and turn it in a clockwise or counterclockwise direction (depending on the desired adjustment) regardless of whether the adjustment-nut appears at the head or at the heel of the guitar.

Remember, you must have full string tension on the neck when measuring the amount of curvature and making these adjustments. The tension of the strings is the primary factor creating the bow.

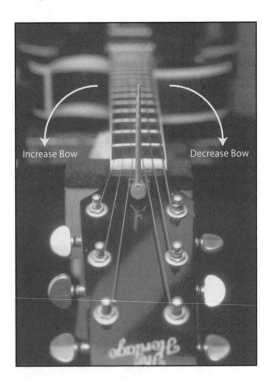

Increase Bow   Decrease Bow

Testing for the Proper Amount of Bow

To test the amount of bow, press down a string simultaneously at the 1st fret and at the fret where the neck joins the body. The amount of bow is the space between that string and the top of the fret lying halfway between the points you are pressing. For example, if your neck joins the body at the 19th fret, put your guitar on a flat surface and touch the 1st and 19th frets simultaneously—the distance between the string and the top of the 9th fret is the amount of bow. You will need a set of feeler gauges to measure this gap.

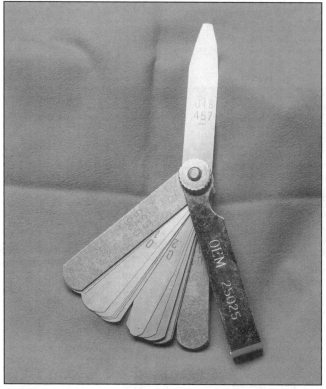

Feeler gauges.

You will need a free hand. You can use a capo to hold the string down at the 1st fret while your other hand touches the string at the point where the neck joins the body, leaving one hand free to measure the bow.

Set the capo just tight enough to touch the strings to the fret. Too much pressure can cause an arch in the string, resulting in a false reading.

To get accurate measurements:

1. String the guitar with the brand and gauge of strings you use.

2. All strings must be on the guitar.

3. The instrument must be tuned to pitch.

Close-up of feeler gauge measuring the distance between fret and string.

Measuring the Amount of Bow

The procedure for measuring the amount of bow is the same for electric, bass, and acoustic guitars, though height specifications will vary. The amount of bow necessary depends on the type and particular characteristics of the instrument, balanced against the needs and demands of the player. However, the following guidelines provide a basic adjustment that will usually suffice:

Having pressed the two points on the string as indicated on page 26, find the midway spot and measure between the string and the top of the fret (the 6th string is usually the most convenient for this). Most repairmen use a mechanic's feeler gauge—the kind used for adjusting points and valves on cars. The following basic standards tend to be the most useful for the widest variety of guitars and playing styles:

For acoustic and electric guitars: .010" (.254 mm).

For bass guitars: .015" (.381 mm).
(See note below.)

NOTE

If slight variations from these specifications are necessary, they can be determined by further experimentation.

In fact, adjusting the truss rod to achieve the correct bow is one area where you may wish merely to understand the process and leave the actual adjustment to a skilled repairman. The amount of adjustment on the truss rod is very critical, and too much movement can either break the rod or cause a back bow. Usually, it takes very little adjustment to arrive at the correct amount of bow. These adjustments change the stresses on the instrument. It is advisable to recheck your measurements after a short period of time, to be sure that the neck has properly settled.

CAUTION

All adjustments should be carried out in small increments and very carefully.

Adjusting the Action at the Bridge

Before you begin to adjust the action at the bridge, the guitar should be strung with the brand and gauge of strings you prefer and tuned to pitch. The degree of tension and specific playing properties of the strings affect action height by stressing the neck.

Necessary Tools

The only tools ordinarily required for these adjustments on electric guitars and basses are:

- Small screwdrivers and/or Allen wrenches of appropriate sizes for the bridge adjustment screws

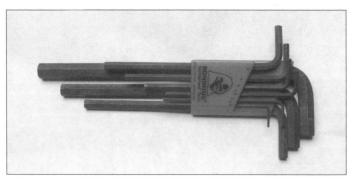

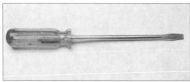

- Studs or set screws (either Allen or slotted type)

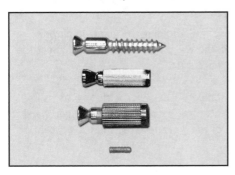

- A scale (ruler)

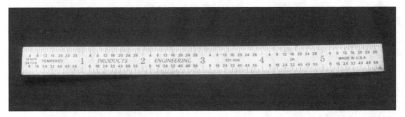

These tools are all available at your music dealer or at hardware stores. Allen wrenches are frequently supplied with the guitar.

Measuring Action Height at the Upper End of the Fingerboard

It is best to make this measurement while holding the guitar in playing position. When resting on a bench, the weight of the guitar may affect the neck position, making the reading inaccurate.

Place the end of a steel rule (a 6" stainless steel ruler with $^1/_{64}$" as its smallest increment) on top of the 12th fret. Look across the fingerboard to measure the gap between the top of the indicated fret and the bottom of the string you are checking.

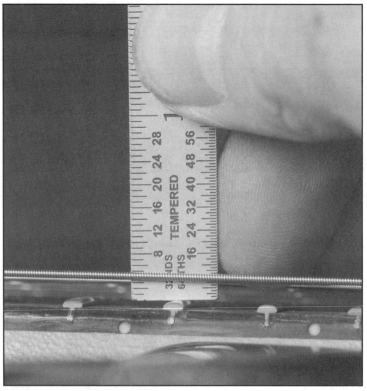

Measuring the action height.

Setup Specifications

Use the chart below to help determine the proper action height for each string of your instrument.

Some players require action that may vary from the chart due to individual playing styles in combination with the variable characteristics of their instrument. The specifications in the chart work well with most instruments and playing styles, and provide a reference to make changes from.

Guitar	String	Action*	Nut Action	Truss Rod
Electrics	1st (high)	4/64" or 1.587 mm	.018" or .457 mm	.010" or .254 mm
	2nd	4/64" or 1.587 mm		
	3rd	4/64" or 1.587 mm		
	4th	4/64" or 1.587 mm		
	5th	5/64" or 1.984 mm		
	6th (low)	5/64" or 1.984 mm		
Acoustics	1st (high)	4/64" or 1.587 mm	.022" or .558 mm	.010" or .254 mm
	2nd	4/64" or 1.587 mm		
	3rd	5/64" or 1.984 mm		
	4th	5/64" or 1.984 mm		
	5th	6/64" or 2.381 mm		
	6th (low)	6/64" or 2.381 mm		
4-String Bass	1st (high)	6/64" or 2.381 mm	.022" or .558 mm	.015" or .381 mm
	2nd	7/64" or 2.778 mm		
	3rd	8/64" or 3.175 mm		
	4th (low)	8/64" or 3.175 mm		
5-String Bass	1st (high)	6/64" or 2.381 mm	.022" or .558 mm	.015" or .381 mm
	2nd	7/64" or 2.778 mm		
	3rd	8/64" or 3.175 mm		
	4th	9/64" or 3.572 mm		
	5th (low)	10/64" or 3.969 mm		
6-String Bass	1st (high)	6/64" or 2.381 mm	.022" or .558 mm	.015" or .381 mm
	2nd	7/64" or 2.778 mm		
	3rd	8/64" or 3.175 mm		
	4th	9/64" or 3.572 mm		
	5th	9/64" or 3.572 mm		
	6th (low)	10/64" or 3.969 mm		
Fretless Bass	1st (high)	6/64" or 2.381 mm	.020" or .508 mm	.010" or .254 mm
	2nd	7/64" or 2.778 mm		
	3rd	8/64" or 3.175 mm		
	4th (low)	8/64" or 3.175 mm		

* Measured at the 12th fret.

Making the Adjustments

Electric guitar bridges have two basic designs. The simplest type has adjustment wheels or studs on each end of a single saddle. It relies on a preset *curvature*.

Curvature refers to the height of the bridge saddles, which are not equal all the way across. Usually, saddles are slightly higher in the middle. This curvature should correspond to the curvature of the fingerboard. By adjusting each end of the bridge to the required specifications, the strings in the middle automatically arrive at the proper specifications.

Adjustments for fixed curvature bridges are done in the following manner:

Step 1: Determine the measurements for the 1st and 6th strings from the setup chart on page 33.

Step 2: Measure the action on your guitar as described on page 32.

Step 3: Adjust the studs or thumb wheels until your guitar matches the specifications. Clockwise rotation of the stud or thumb wheel lowers the action, and counterclockwise movement raises it.

CAUTION

Some stud-type bridges have locking screws that should be released before making height adjustments. Your owner's manual will tell you how to do this.

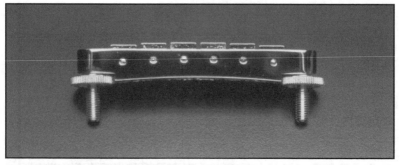

Thumb-wheel bridge.

The other type of bridge has individually adjustable saddles. Each saddle must be adjusted for the proper clearance from the fret.

Adjustments for bridges with individual saddles are done in the following manner:

Step 1: Determine the measurements for the 1st through 6th strings from the setup chart on page 33.

Step 2: Measure the action on your guitar as described on page 32.

Step 3: Adjust both screws so the saddle remains parallel to the base plate. This will maintain proper string spacing.

Usually, with this type of bridge, clockwise rotation raises the string and counterclockwise rotation lowers the string.

Adjustments for electric basses are done the same way but with different specifications (see page 33).

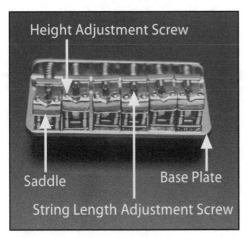

Bridge with individual saddles.

Adjusting the Action at the Nut

After setting the action at the bridge, the next step is to set the action at the nut. Remember, the guitar should be strung with the brand and gauge of strings you prefer and tuned to pitch.

Bone, Plastic, or Graphite Nuts
Necessary Tools

To measure action height at the nut, you should use the same feeler gauge set you used for measuring the truss rod adjustment. You will require gauge blades between .018" (.457 mm) to .022" (.559 mm).

Adjusting the action at the nut involves actually cutting the nut slots deeper. For this, you can use X-acto saws for the treble strings and nut files for the bass strings. X-acto saws are available from hobby shops, hardware stores or luthier's suppliers. The nut file is a specialized guitar repairman's tool. They are available from luthier's suppliers or industrial suppliers. Both X-acto saws and nut files come in varying widths to accommodate different string gauges. It is necessary to select a blade or file that is slightly wider than the string to prevent the string from binding in the nut.

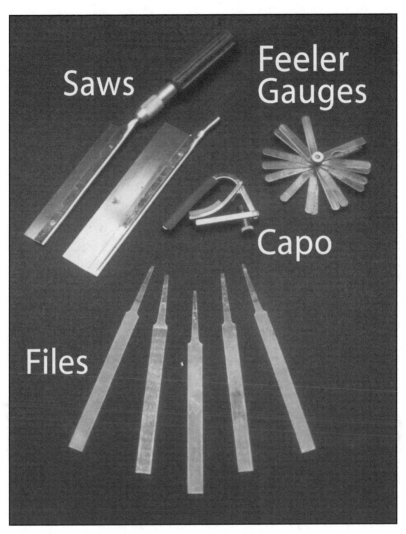

Tools necessary for adjusting action at the nut.

Measuring Action at the 1st Fret

Measurements to determine proper action at the nut are done with a feeler gauge at the 1st fret. Hold the gauge parallel to the string surface to get an accurate measurement.

Step 1: Select the proper feeler gauge blade from the specification chart on page 33.

Step 2: Insert the blade between the string and the 1st fret. You must hold the gauge parallel to the string surface to ensure an accurate measurement. (See photo to the right.)

For electric guitars, .018" (.4572 mm) between the 1st fret and the bottom of each string is usually an ideal height—low enough to be comfortable but high enough to avoid buzzing. For basses and acoustic guitars, use .022" (.5588 mm).

Lower or higher settings than these may be used, depending on the instrument's resonance factor, structural strength, type of strings used, etc., but these recommended heights will work well for most players.

Measuring the nut action.

Re-Slotting to Specifications

Step 1: Check the nut height (measured at the 1st fret).

Step 2: If the string is too high, you must carefully re-slot the nut deeper by cutting with an X-acto saw or file.

Step 3: Re-measure and cut until the feeler gauge touches both fret and string yet does not push the string upward. The fit should be exact.

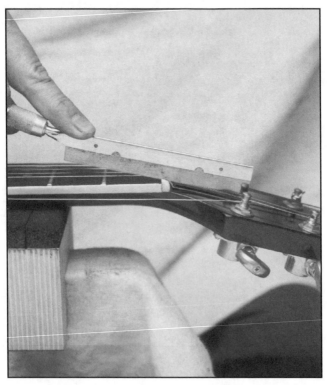

Cut the groove deeper for the treble strings with an X-acto saw.

Cut the groove deeper for the bass strings with a nut file.

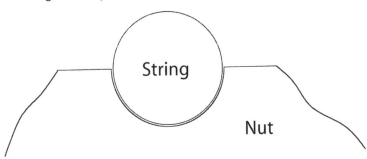

String

Nut

The fit should be exact.

Important Rules

Rule 1: Remember, it takes very little cutting to lower the string! Unfortunately, it's easier to remove material (by cutting too deep) than it is to replace it.

Rule 2: The angle of the nut slot is very important. The nut slots should be cut at the same angle as that of the string from the nut to the capstan. This will ensure proper downward pressure and that the string departs properly from the edge of the nut facing the fingerboard. (See photo to the right).

Rule 3: Proceed cautiously, cutting small amounts and then re-measuring. Repeat the process until the adjustment is correct. Remember to restore full tension to the string each time you re-measure.

Rule 4: **Remember!** Make sure the string is fully seated in the slot each time you take a measurement. If your saw or file sizing isn't correct, the string may wedge above the bottom of the slot resulting in a flawed measurement. If you don't notice this and keep cutting, you will make the slot too deep and ruin the nut.

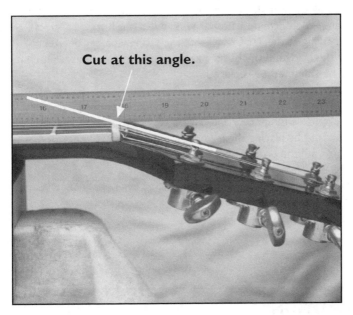

Cut at this angle.

The nut slots should be cut at the same angle that the string creates from the nut to the capstan.

If the Slot Is Too Deep—Shimming the Nut

Buzzes caused by the nut slot being too low occur only when the string is played open. To determine whether you have a nut buzz or a saddle buzz, press a string at the 1st fret so that the string vibrates between that fret and the bridge. If the buzz is gone, you have a nut buzz. The nut may have to be shimmed or replaced.

Putting glue in the slots to shim up the string is not recommended. This makeshift approach is temporary and unreliable. It is more advisable to raise the entire nut by placing shims under it and regluing it in position, then reslotting until the proper height is achieved for all strings.

Shims are typically made of plastic, sheet metal, or even heavy paper, such as pieces of file folder material.

CAUTION

An expert should remove a bone, plastic, or graphite nut for shimming. Attempts by the inexperienced often cause irreparable damage to the nut channel or to the finish surrounding it.

Mechanical Nuts

Electric guitars with mechanical nuts require different adjustment procedures. Adjustments are made by adding or removing shims under the nut assembly.

The Measurements for Mechanical Nuts

Step 1: Measure and record the height of each string from the 1st fret.

Step 2: Note if the strings are all the same height from the 1st fret. This will help to determine if the nut follows the curvature of the fingerboard. If the middle strings are closer to the 1st fret than the outside two, the nut doesn't conform to the curvature.

Interpreting the Measurements

1. If the nut is too high, subtract the standard specification from the measured overage. This will be the amount of shim you will have to remove.

2. Conversely, if the nut height is too low, some shims will have to be added until the proper specification is reached.

3. In the case where the curvature of the nut doesn't conform to the curvature of the neck, the action must be adjusted using the height specification of the lowest string.

4. If the strings conform to the fingerboard, the action can be adjusted by adding or removing shims to each end until the proper height is achieved.

5. If the nut is too high with no shims, it will be necessary to remove wood from the nut slot. **To avoid cosmetic damage to the instrument, an expert should do this.**

Mechanical nuts.

Making the Adjustments

For a guitar without a locking trem, go directly to Step 2.

Step 1: On a guitar with a locking trem, loosen and remove nut locks.

Step 2: Loosen the strings until slack. (If you have a floating trem, don't forget the spacer at the bridge!)

Step 3: Loosen and remove the screws on the back of the neck that hold the nut assembly.

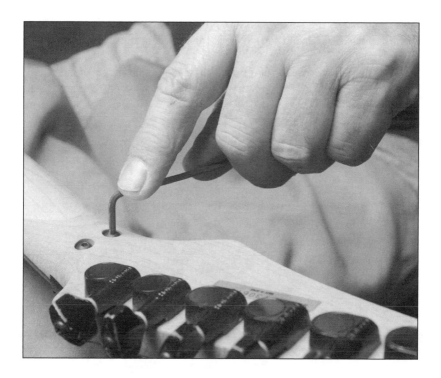

Step 4: Carefully remove the nut assembly, noting the position and height of existing shims. (See photo on the following page.)

Step 5: Add or subtract the appropriate shims to arrive at the proper specification.

Step 6: Reattach the nut assembly and tune the strings to pitch. Stretch and retune. Lock the nut clamps.

Industrial supply stores sell shim stock. It is made of thin sheets of metal that can be cut with scissors. It comes in varying thicknesses, calibrated to a thousandth of an inch.

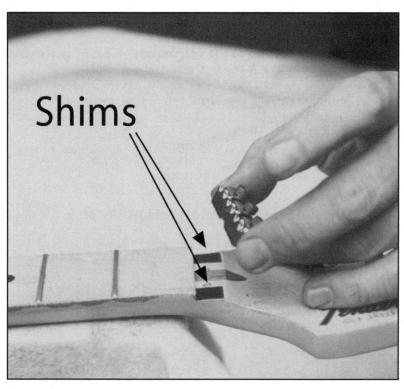

Placing shims under the nut.

Intonation

It is not unusual for guitarists to find that, despite their best efforts, their guitar will not play in tune. It may be in tune in the open position but in higher positions one or all of the strings are out of tune. This frustrating situation is usually related to the vibrating string length, which is measured from the nut to the bridge.

This section is about how to check your intonation and change the string length to correct it.

Basic Principles of String Length

1. Too short a string length will cause a string to be sharp (sound slightly higher in pitch) as you move up into higher positions.

2. Too long a string length will cause a string to go flat (sound slightly lower in pitch) as you move up into higher positions.

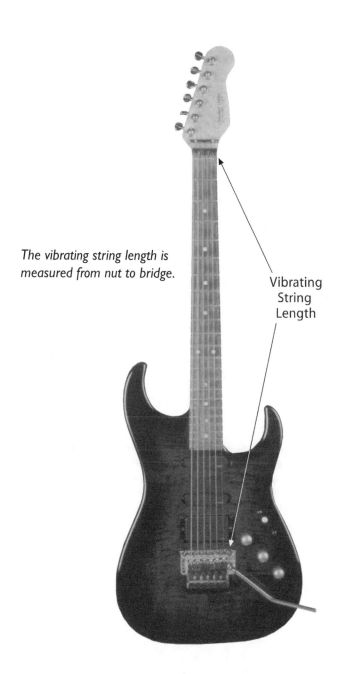

The vibrating string length is measured from nut to bridge.

Vibrating
String
Length

Electronic Tuners

There are several types of electronic tuning devices that can be used for checking intonation. They translate the incoming signal (i.e., musical note) into a visual image that accurately indicates whether the note being played is on pitch, sharp, or flat.

Basic Rules of Operation:

1. When the note being played is on pitch, the indicator holds on center.

2. Movement to the left indicates flatness.

3. Movement to the right indicates sharpness.

Tuners work in various ways. The most commonly used tuners use a *sample and hold* technology, meaning the signal is sampled several times, analyzed, and then displayed. Sample and hold–type tuners include:

Meter: which has a needle that stands up straight if the signal is in tune.

Light pulsation or stroboscopic: which has a row of lights that lock in the center when the signal is in tune.

Cathode ray tube tuner (see page 56 for an explanation).

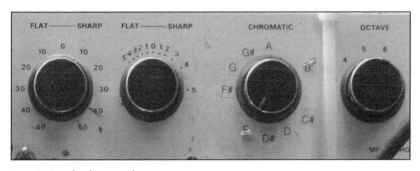

Detail of cathode ray tube tuner.

Since these tuners are sampling several times before displaying results, they do not work in real time—the results are delayed. Other less commonly used tuners work in real time. They include:

Cathode Ray Tube: which has a square pattern that locks in the middle of a screen when the signal is in tune.

Stroboscopic: which displays a rotating disc on a screen that appears to stop when in tune.

On stroboscopic tuners, the speed of movement to the right or left indicates the relative degree of sharpness or flatness. If the indicator moves very quickly to the left, the intonation is more flat. If the indicator moves very slowly to the left, the intonation is less flat. Due to the device's extreme sensitivity to the slightest irregularities in the string, there may be small movements around the center point of the indicator even when the string is in tune. When the string is in tune, the movement is equidistant from the center.

An assortment of strobe tuners.

Reasons to Use an Electronic Tuner

Electronic tuning devices are far more accurate than the human ear because they:

1. Detect much smaller frequency changes.

2. Register only the actual pitch of the note, while the ear often has difficulty because tone quality and overtones obscure pitch.

3. Are a consistent reference for *absolute pitch*.

Absolute pitch refers to the exact frequency of a note. In other words, "A" is "A" because it is 440 Hz (hertz, or cycles per second). Relative pitch has to do with how one note compares to another.

The stroboscopic devices are usually accurate to within one *cent* (1/100 of a *half step*). A half step is the distance of one fret. Even some of the simpler and less expensive devices are accurate to within five cents.

If you frequently do your own intonation adjustments, a quality tuning device can be a worthwhile investment. They are also very useful for general tuning, especially on stage where ambient sound can make it difficult to hear whether or not you are in tune.

Typical sample and hold–type electronic tuning devices.

Finger Pressure and Intonation

Be careful not to press too hard. Applying too much pressure to a string can stretch it downward into the fingerboard. This makes the pitch go sharp. Misplacement of the fingers on the strings can also cause you to pull the string slightly off center, as in bending a string, with the same undesirable result. Proper finger pressure is just enough so that the string touches the fret firmly. Remember to place your fingers in close proximity to the fret. This will give you the leverage you need to secure the string against the fret without pressing too hard. To learn proper finger pressure, try this experiment:

Step 1: In normal playing position, place a finger on the 6th (lowest) string in close proximity to the 5th fret, *but do not press. Just lightly touch the string.*

Step 2: Begin to apply pressure very slowly, in small increments, plucking all the while. At first, you will produce unpitched percussive sounds. Then, you will produce a slightly buzzy, unclear tone.

Step 3: The next tiny increment of pressure you apply should get you a clear, ringing sound.

NOTE

The steps above demonstrate how hard you need to press any note! Pressing harder will cause your notes to sound sharp!

Excess finger pressure may cause the string to be displaced and sound sharp.

Testing and Adjusting Intonation

Tips for Using Tuning Devices to Test Intonation

Step 1: Before using the tuning device, be sure it is properly
calibrated (follow the manufacturer's directions).

Step 2: Install new strings (see page 12). As strings get old, they
become corroded, filled or covered with body oils, and
dented by the frets. All of these factors inhibit normal vibration
of the string and cause false readings.

Step 3: Lower the pickups away from the strings to avoid excess
magnetic pull. Magnetic pull can cause erratic string vibration,
making it impossible to achieve proper intonation.

Step 4: Pre-tune the guitar to concert pitch (A = 440). This step
is important for two reasons:

1) It is necessary to have full tension on the neck when making
adjustments since tension affects action and therefore intonation.

2) A string that is not tuned to correct pitch may produce a false
reading on the tuner. Some tuning devices pick up and register
harmonic overtones. For example, if the tuner is set to "E," a
string tuned accidentally to "A" could produce a stable pattern
on the indicator because "A" is a natural overtone of "E." By
pre-tuning the guitar, you ensure that the indicator is registering
the proper note.

Step 5: Hold the guitar in normal playing position when testing
intonation. Holding the guitar adds slight stresses to the neck
and body and these stresses affect intonation. Testing in this
way ensures adjustments that compensate for playing conditions.

Step 6: For electric guitars and basses, use a standard patch cord to plug directly into the tuning device. Set the pickup selector switch to the neck position and volume and tone controls to the full position. This will ensure maximum signal. For acoustic guitars, you can use the tuner's internal microphone.

Step 7: Use the 12th fret harmonic instead of the open string when tuning with the device. The harmonic creates more vibrations per second, causing a more continuous signal and therefore a clearer signal.

NOTE

With tuners that have auto-seek, one need only be concerned with tuning to the proper octave.

Now that you know about tuners and finger pressure, and have followed the steps as described on pages 60–61, you are ready to test and correct your intonation.

The Test—Part I

Step 1: Play the harmonic at the 12th fret. Tune the string until the tuner registers proper pitch.

Step 2: Play the note at the 12th fret of the string you just tuned. *Do not press too hard!* Take note if the string registers sharp or flat on the tuner. Do this several times to get the best average.

The Adjustment

If the fretted note is flat, the string is too long and must be shortened. If the fretted note is sharp, the string is too short and must be lengthened. To change the string length, you must adjust the saddle intonation screw. Clockwise rotation lengthens the string, and counterclockwise shortens the string.

Setting the string length adjustment screw (intonation). Be careful not to damage the front of the guitar with the shaft of the screwdriver.

On some bridges, there may be a saddle lock screw that must be released before making adjustments.

On Floyd Rose–style systems, the string must be de-tuned before loosening the saddle lock screw. Set the string length adjustment and re-lock prior to retuning.

On some other bridges without intonation adjustment screws, loosen the saddle lock screws, move the saddle to the correct position, and lock in place.

The Test—Part 2

Step 3: Retune the string to the open 12th fret harmonic and repeat Steps 1 and 2. When the open 12th fret harmonic and the fretted octave are the same, the intonation is on.

Step 4: Repeat Steps 1 through 3 on the rest of the strings.

NOTE

Thin strings flex right at the saddle, while stiffer strings don't. Because of this physical property, stiff strings must be longer to play in tune.

Acoustic Guitars

Unfortunately, most acoustic guitars can't be adjusted in the way that was just described for electric guitars. To change the string length, a repairman may have to alter or move the saddle to a different position. This kind of work can be further complicated on acoustic guitars with pickups under or built into the saddle. You can test your acoustic guitar intonation but you should let a professional fix it!

Cleaning and Polishing
Your Guitar

Caring for your guitar's finish is a relatively simple procedure, but one which must be carried out with the proper materials and an understanding of their use. Prior to restringing is an appropriate time to polish your guitar (see page 9–11). Periodic maintenance of the finish enhances the beauty of the instrument. It also helps to prevent permanent surface damage that may result from the cumulative effects of wear and grime.

The two areas of concern in finish maintenance are:

1. The finished surfaces of the neck and body.

2. The unfinished surface of the fingerboard.

This section will discuss cleaning of these surfaces and the application of appropriate waxes and polishes for protection and preservation.

CAUTION

Be sure to read and understand these procedures before applying any unknown or new substances to your guitar.

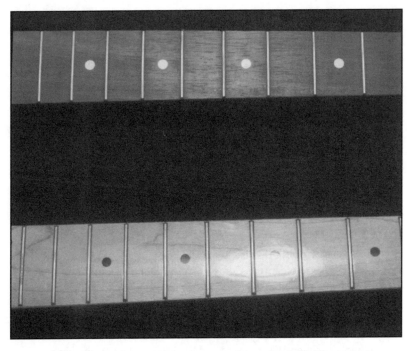

Some necks are unfinished (top) and others are finished (bottom).

Types of Finishes

Guitars and other fretted instruments are finished with a variety of protective substances, the most common of which are nitrocellulose lacquer and synthetic finishes such as polyurethanes and polyesters. Most of these finishes are subject to oxidation and fading; all are subject to abrasion and the buildup of residues on the surface (grime, perspiration, wax, and smoke films).

If these effects are not dealt with regularly, they may lead to unnecessary and permanent damage to the guitar's finish.

Choosing the Correct Cleaning Solvent and Polish

Using a solvent or polish that is chemically incompatible with a given finish may cause irreparable damage. Some guitar and furniture polishes contain cleaning solvents as well as polishing and waxing agents; it is unsafe to assume that a polish will not react with the finish.

Probably 95% of contemporary guitars are finished either in nitrocellulose lacquer or synthetics and lend themselves to the basic methods described here for cleaning and polishing. By testing first, you can avoid noticeable damage to the instrument from a reaction between the finish and the substance applied to it.

Testing Solvents, Cleaners, and Polishes

Whatever the substance—water, chemical solvent, cleaning compound, wax, or polish—test it on a small section of the guitar before working over the entire surface. For example, you can choose a small spot under a back plate or truss rod cover to test whether there will be a reaction between the substance and the finish. With the vast majority of guitars, it is highly unlikely that there will be any problem. In the rare case where there is a reaction, using this approach will assure that the damage will be slight. The chances of a reaction are extremely remote, but it is easier to be cautious in the first place than to correct substantial damage in the rare instance it does occur.

> **CAUTION**
>
> *Various manufacturers make "guitar polish," and such products are available at most music stores. Be very careful and do not assume that these are "safe." Test them carefully before committing to their use. It is a good idea to put a dab of the substance on a cloth instead of applying it directly to your guitar. Then, test it as described above.*

Polishing Cloths

All cleaning and polishing should be done with flannelette, a soft cotton material available at fabric stores. Do not use pre-treated flannelette cloths—they may harm the finish. Avoid using ordinary rag material or paper towels, as they may have an undesirable abrasive quality.

Step 1: Fold the cloth into a small pad for applying the solvent, cleaner, or polish.

Step 2: Always do one section at a time, wiping it immediately with a clean, dry piece of cloth.

Flannelette can be washed and re-used, although washing lessens its softness.

Make sure that the cloths are free of debris, such as wood or metal particles, that might scratch the guitar's surface. Cloth used for one cleaning or polishing operation should not be used for another.

For example, a cloth used with cleaning compounds will contain abrasives that will interfere with subsequent polishing and waxing.

Use a flannelette cloth to polish your guitar.

Preliminary Cleaning with Damp and Dry Cloths

In most cases, some of the accumulated substances on the finished surface are water soluble, while others require a chemical solvent or cleaning compound.

As a matter of procedure, it is best to first carefully clean the surface with water before using chemical solvents or compounds.

One method is to slightly dampen a flannelette cloth and clean the finish one small section at a time, wiping immediately with a dry cloth after each application.

Clean one small section at a time.

Cleaning Lacquer and Synthetic Finishes with Chemical Solvents

After completing the steps explained on pages 72–73, repeat the procedure using mineral spirits to dampen the flannelette cloth. Work on a small section at a time and clean it with a fresh dry cloth. Be sure to remove all residue before moving onto the next section. Mineral spirits are available at hardware and paint stores.

CAUTION

Always use solvents sparingly and carefully. Follow the safety instructions on the container.

Occasionally, the application of a chemical solvent will result in a thin hazy film on the surface of the guitar. This is usually due to oxidation or a wax residue that is resistant to the solvent. In such a case, the haze can be removed by application of cleaning compounds in accordance with the instructions on pages 70–71.

Removing Oxides and Abrasions from Lacquered and Synthetic Finishes

In many cases, cleaning with water and chemical solvents will be sufficient to prepare the surface for final polishing or waxing. Sometimes, oxidation of the finish has dulled it to such an extent that wax or polish alone will not restore it to a high luster, or there may be minor abrasions that mark its appearance.

After cleaning the entire finished surface of the instrument with water and solvent, you can determine the state of the finish. Oxidation or minor abrasions can be handled with a cleaning compound.

> **CAUTION**
>
> *Deep marks, dents, abrasions, or scratches*
>
> *cannot be removed in this manner. Such*
>
> *problems require expert attention—*
>
> *refinishing in most cases.*

An excellent agent for removing minor abrasions or oxides and restoring depth and luster is any mild polishing compound that contains both mild abrasives and polishing agents. Reputable brands are available at auto supply and hardware stores.

Step 1: Place just a bit of compound on a flannelette cloth and work it over the finish, covering a small area at a time.

Step 2: Wipe immediately with a clean, dry flannelette cloth. Use small circular motions on solid colors; rub with the grain where it is visible. The amount of pressure should be light to moderate, depending on the severity of the problem to be corrected.

Step 3: Apply a second application of the compound, using lighter pressure. This will reduce the rubbing marks created by abrasives in the first application.

The compound will always leave small marks, but these should fill in when the polish or wax is applied.

Nevertheless, use the compound sparingly and carefully, remembering that it removes a very thin layer of finish in order to expose fresh gloss.

Make sure all residues are removed before polishing and waxing. The use of a cleaning compound should be necessary no more than once every one or two years, depending on the guitar and its use. Exercise some restraint in deciding when to apply it. For example, if only one section of the guitar needs this treatment, refrain from using the compound on all the surfaces merely as a matter of routine, and apply it only when necessary.

Waxing and Polishing

Once the finish has been cleaned, gloss can be further restored and heightened with a high quality guitar or furniture polish. This will leave a strong shine that both enhances and protects the finish. Spray waxes and polishes are easy to use since you can spray a small amount onto the flannelette cloth and apply directly, but other liquid waxes and polishes are equally effective. Apply the polish sparingly, covering a small area at a time. Use different cloths for cleaning and polishing.

Fingerboards with lacquer or synthetic finishes should be cleaned and polished with the same methods described above.

Cleaning and Polishing the Unfinished Fingerboard

Most unfinished fingerboards are made of rosewood or ebony. They should not be cleaned and polished in the same way finished fingerboards are, since raw wood requires special treatment. Certain substances contained in polishes and cleaners need to be avoided.

To clean the fingerboard, and to shine the frets simultaneously, use 0000 grade steel wool. This is the finest grade available.

CAUTION

Do <u>not</u> use a coarser grade than

0000 steel wool.

Work the steel wool across the fingerboard and frets, scrubbing perpendicular to the length of the neck. Be careful that the steel wool touches only the surface of the fingerboard and not the headstock, the finished portion of the neck or the body of the instrument. On electric guitars, put masking tape across the tops of the pickups so that the iron particles from the steel wool will not attach to the magnetic pole pieces (the particles may affect the functioning of the pickups).

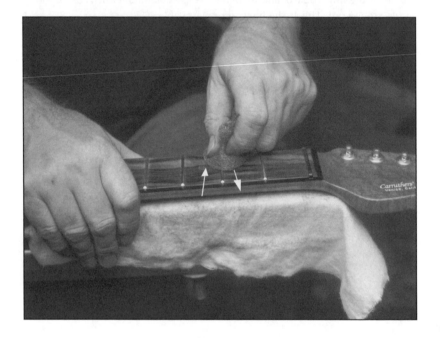

Once the fingerboard is cleaned, the natural oils from the hands will lightly polish it in the course of playing. In most cases, this is all that is needed. However, if extra smoothness is desired, carnauba paste wax can be used on the fingerboard. Apply it in accordance with the directions provided with the product.

CAUTION

Never leave steel wool near a 9-volt battery

as it can easily ignite.

Routine Cleaning

You can reduce the need for revitalizing the finish by keeping the guitar in its case, wiping it down with a clean flannelette cloth after playing, and avoiding exposure of the instrument to the elements. These practices should be followed with all types of guitars.

Electronic Maintenance

Electric guitars and basses are subject to electronic problems. The most common problems are loose components, such as the jack or potentiometers, and corrosion.

In the case of loose components, the wires often break off due to fatigue caused by loose components moving around, such as potentiometers or jacks. To restore normal function, the wires must be reconnected. This is usually done by soldering.

In the case of corrosion, the components must be cleaned and lubricated or replaced.

Soldering

Soldering is a distinct form of low-temperature welding that provides a bond between two metal surfaces. Unlike some types of welding that fuse metals together, solder only fills in the spaces in and between adjacent metals. Solder is used to make a reliable electrical connection that will remain free from corrosion and have good *conductance* (the ability of a material to conduct electricity).

Most people know what soldering is, but very few know how to do it properly.

Basic Requirements for Soldering

1. The correct materials

2. Proper tools

3. Good preparation

4. Correct technique

Qualities of Solders

Solders are mixtures of low melting-point metals such as tin and lead. Varying the ratio of the different metals controls the melting point of the solder. Usually the solder has a core that is made from rosin. This cleans the metals to be joined and promotes the proper flow.

Solders come in different diameters. Normally the diameter is selected according to the size of the job. For example, if you were soldering on an intricate circuit board, you would want to use small diameter solder.

NOTE
Some solders have acid cores. This is undesirable for electrical connections.

Necessary Tools for Soldering

1. A high quality soldering iron of the appropriate wattage (anywhere from 25 to 40 watts will take care of most guitar-related repairs).

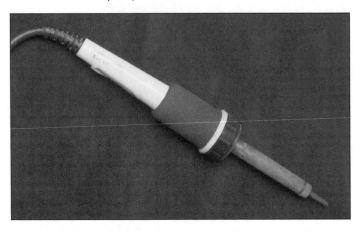

2. A cellulose sponge (for cleaning the tip of the soldering iron).

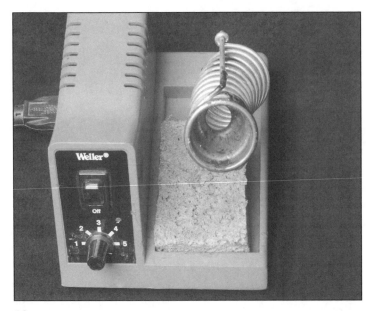

3. Wire strippers.

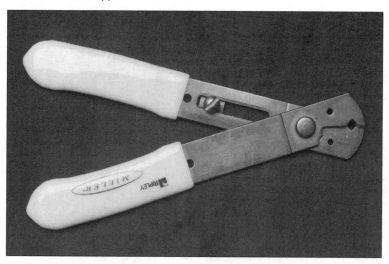

4. Soldering aids (needle-nose pliers, clamps, a vise, etc.).

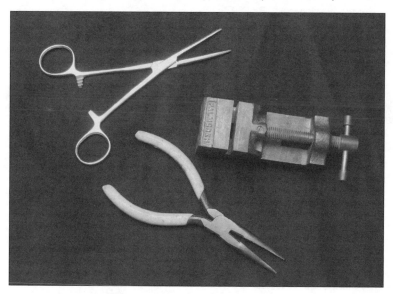

5. High quality solder.

6. Heat shrink tubing (insulating connections) and a butane lighter for heating it.

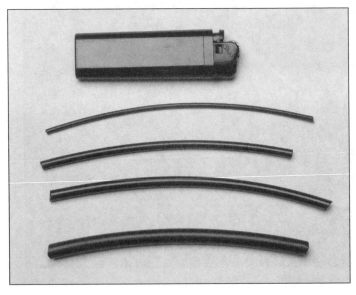

Proper Preparation

One of the primary rules of soldering is cleanliness. Dirt, corrosion, oils, or other types of contaminants interfere with the bonding process.

Preparation for Soldering:

1. Make sure that the surfaces to be joined are as clean as possible. You can use a fine sandpaper to clean them.

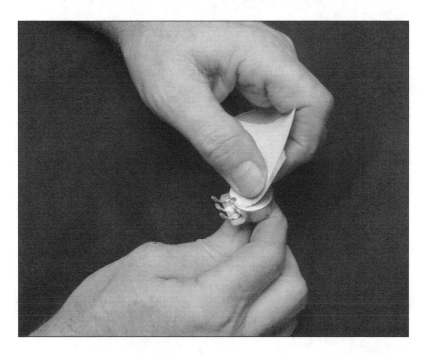

2. Insulation on the wire must be stripped back with wire strippers.

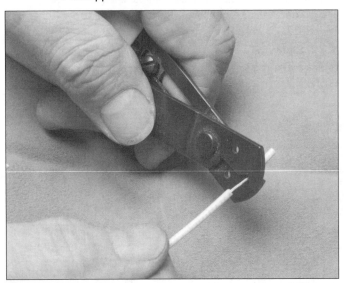

3. The pieces to be soldered must be held in close proximity to each other.

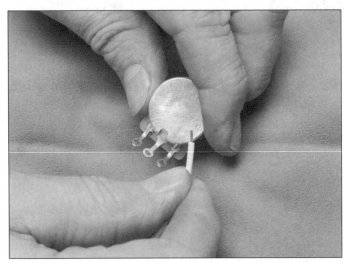

NOTE

Soldering aids are very useful for holding and positioning the parts to be soldered. Be sure that the aids are not located too close to the joint area, as they will dissipate heat and make soldering more difficult.

CAUTION

Soldering irons and molten solder are very hot. To avoid being burned or damaging the finish on your guitar, caution should be used in handling this equipment. Place thin cardboard shields over areas of the guitar that could be exposed to damage.

An ounce of prevention is worth a pound of cure!

The Soldering Process

Step 1: Before attempting to solder, it is very important to clean the soldering iron tip. Let your iron come to full temperature, then wipe the tip on a damp cellulose sponge.

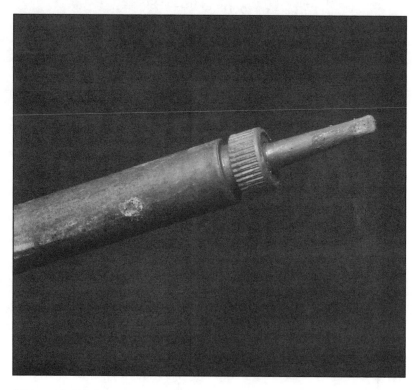

Dirty soldering iron.

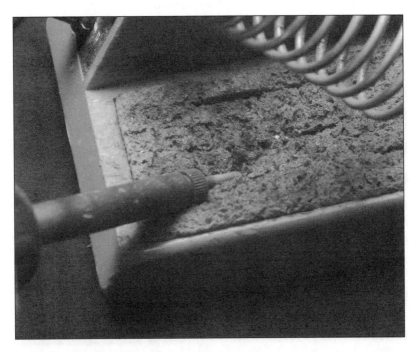

Cleaning the soldering iron.

Step 2: To facilitate easier soldering, pre-coat each part with solder. Use the tip of the iron to apply heat directly to the metal being soldered. Touch the solder to a heated part.

When the part is hot enough, the solder will melt and coat it. This should be done to both surfaces prior to joining. This process is known as *tinning*.

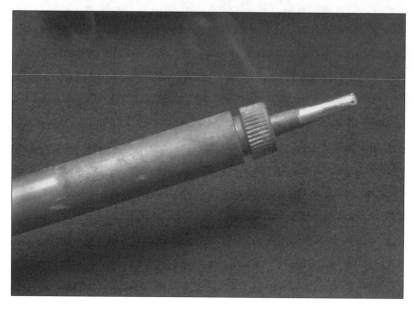

Tin the soldering iron.

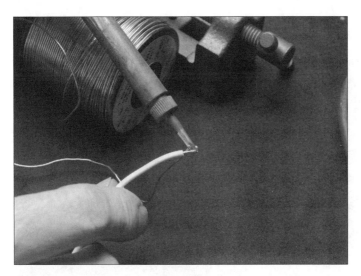

Tin the stripped wire.

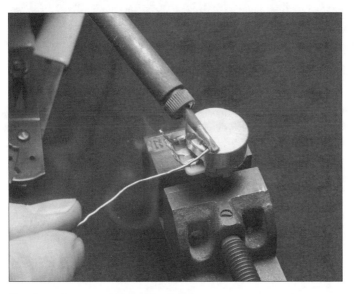

Tin the other part. Notice the handy vise.

Step 3: Place both parts in close proximity to each other and apply
heat to both simultaneously.

Sometimes, it is necessary to apply a little more solder to get a good joint.

Be careful not to move the parts until the solder has cooled.
Remember, the closer the proximity the better the joint.

The most common problem with soldering is a *cold joint*. This is caused by not getting the metals to be joined to a high enough temperature. The other common problem is a bad joint due to dirty surfaces.

In addition to repairing connections, your newly acquired soldering skills can be used to install new pickups, *active electronics* (circuitry that requires batteries), or repair patch cords.

Insulation

In some cases, it may be necessary to insulate splices or solder joints that come in close proximity to other components. This is best accomplished with the use of *heat shrink tubing*. Heat shrink tubing is an insulating material that comes in different diameters and colors. Prior to soldering, pick a piece of tubing long enough to cover the affected area. Slip the tubing over the wire. Make sure it is far enough back to avoid premature shrinkage from heat caused by the soldering iron. After the joint has cooled, slide the shrink tubing over the joint and apply a heat source, such as a butane lighter.

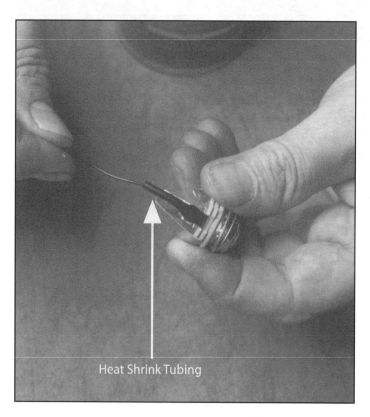

Heat Shrink Tubing

Cleaning and Lubricating Components

Potentiometers ("pots"—the dials you turn to adjust tone and volume) and switches are subject to corrosion. You may have noticed a crackling sound when you turn the knobs or activate switches. This can be very aggravating. In many cases, a simple cleaning and lubricating is all that is necessary. Electronic stores carry contact spray cleaners and lubricants.

The cleaning and lubricating process is as follows:

Step 1: Insert the extension tube into the spray nozzle.

Step 2: Insert the extension tube into the opening in the pot casing and spray. Rotate the knob several times in quick succession.

Step 3: Repeat this procedure with the lubricant.

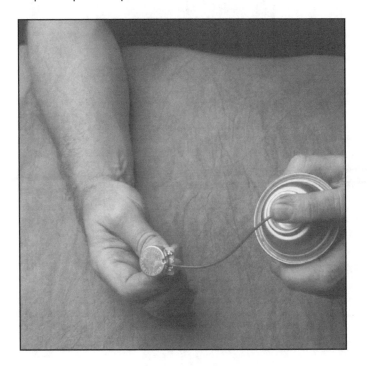

Your Setup

By now, you may have experimented and decided on exactly the right setup for each of your instruments. Here is a chart for you to fill in and keep track of this information. Use a pencil, as you may change your mind from time to time.

Have fun!

Guitar	String	Action	Nut Action	Truss Rod

SETTING UP AND ADJUSTING YOUR FLOYD ROSE SYSTEM

Introduction

Many players, inspired by the "whammy masters," rushed out and purchased guitars equipped with Floyd Rose tremolo systems of one kind or another. Unfortunately, they receive little or no information on the proper use and maintenance of the product.

Floyd Rose tremolos can create some miraculous effects in the hands of the right player. They can also be a nightmare. The first time you break a string and find that your whole guitar has gone out of tune in the middle of a performance can be more than a little disconcerting. This is why it is important to understand and maintain your system for maximum performance and reliability. The simplest operation, such as restringing, can turn into a disaster resulting in a trip to the guitar repair shop. Hardly a week goes by in my shop without a new guitar owner coming in with a minor disaster. Adjusting the action and intonation are tasks that players should be able to do for themselves.

After many years of experience working on instruments, we have written this section to enlighten players and technicians alike about working on guitars equipped with Floyd Rose tremolos.

Even if you prefer to have a tech work on your guitar, it doesn't hurt to know what's involved.

Hopefully, you will agree this section is presented in a clear, step-by-step manner and arranged in the proper sequence to obtain optimal results. We have included many photos, drawings, and charts to further enhance your understanding. Finally, we have included a diagnostic section to help pinpoint specific problems and their solutions.

Our sincerest wish is make your playing more enjoyable and a lot less complicated.

History of the Modern Tremolo

The early tremolos were designed in the late '40s and early '50s by people like Paul Bigsby and Leo Fender. The name "tremolo" was a misnomer for "vibrato." Vibrato is a change in pitch. Tremolo is a change in volume. However, through constant misuse, the name tremolo became the accepted name.

Early tremolos were okay for subtle effects but caused tuning problems when overused.

Beginnings of the Floyd Rose Tremolo

Floyd Rose, a young guitarist machinist, could see that players like Eddie Van Halen, Steve Vai, Brad Gillis, and many others were experiencing difficulty keeping their guitars in tune when using their conventional tremolo systems to the extreme. As a result, he designed the original version of the Floyd Rose tremolo in the 1970s.

Floyd Rose decided that he could improve the original Fender design. He found several problems in the original design. The strings moved across the nut and bridge saddles when the tremolo was activated. When the tremolo returned to the neutral position the strings didn't. The method for pivoting the bridge assembly was crude and involved too much friction. These factors made it nearly impossible to keep the guitar in tune. He decided to lock the strings at the nut and the bridge. Then he used a knife-edge pivot to eliminate friction.

The early models didn't have fine tuners. This made trying to get the guitar in tune very difficult. The player had to guess how much to detune the guitar to compensate for the sharping or flattening effect of the nut clamps when they were tightened. To deal with this problem, a new model was designed that had fine tuners. It could be tuned after the strings were locked.

The next significant modification was to lower the position of the fine tuners so that a player's hand wouldn't put the guitar out of tune by resting against the bridge assembly.

With these improvements, the Floyd Rose tremolo proved to hold tune better than any other tremolo system.

Due to the effectiveness of the Floyd Rose system, many manufacturers licensed the design and came out with their own versions. They include Fender, Gotoh, Ibanez, Schaller, Takeuchi, Yamaha, and many others.

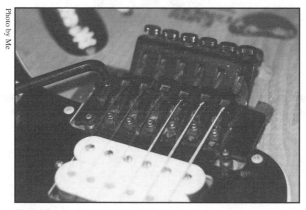

Floyd Rose–licensed tremolo system by Gotoh.

Features

The Floyd Rose tremolo features:

    1. A locking nut.

2. Locking saddles.

3. Knife-edge pivots.

4. Fine tuners.

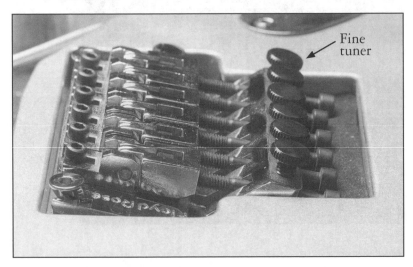

Fine
tuner

Understanding the Basic Principles of Operation

Before you can use the Floyd Rose tremolo properly, you must understand how the system works. The principles that make the Floyd Rose tremolo stay in tune also make setting up, stringing, and playing different than conventional tremolos.

The Floyd Rose tremolo works on the same principle as a balance beam scale. The tension of the strings (on one side of the scale) is offset by the springs (on the other side of the scale). If you change string tension, then you must adjust the springs to match. This is what makes the Floyd Rose tremolo extremely sensitive.

NOTE

Tension can be affected by increasing or decreasing string gauge, or by tuning above or below normal pitch.

On the facing page is an illustration of the parts of a Floyd Rose system. Each part is labeled with a number. The names of the parts, and their corresponding numbers, are listed below.

#	Parts Description
1	Fine tuner
2	String lock bolts
3	Base plate mounting bolt
4	Saddle lock bolt
5	Clamp blocks
6	Saddle assembly
7	Knife-edge pivot
8	Pivot stud (wood screw base)
9	Pivot stud (machine bolt)
10	Pivot stud body insert
11	Fine tuner spring assembly
12	Sustain block
13	Springs
14	Claw mounting screws
15	Claw
16	String retainer assembly
17	Nut mounting bolts
18	Lock washers
19	Nut shim
20	Nut
21	Nut caps
22	Nut lock bolts
23	Tremolo arm bushing
24	Base plate
25	Tremolo arm

Nut-Related Parts — (bracket spanning rows 16 through 22)

Floyd Rose System Parts

See page 106 for part names.

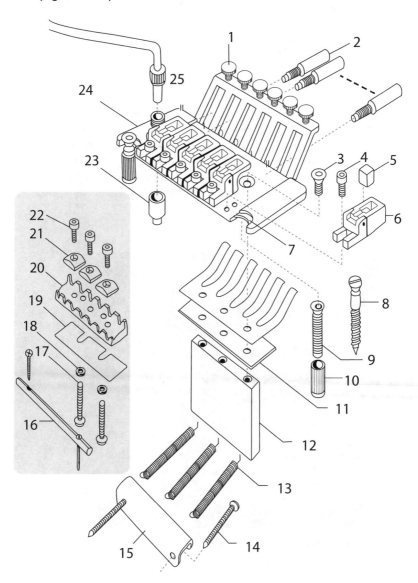

Stringing Your Floyd Rose Tremolo

The first step to setting up and adjusting your Floyd Rose tremolo is to learn how to properly install the strings.

Steps for Removal:

Step 1: Insert spacer under back of tremolo. Push the tremolo arm in to insert a spacer just thick enough to keep the tremolo in level position between the face of the guitar and the bottom of the tremolo. Use a material that won't damage the guitar's finish (for example, bottle cork). This will stabilize the tremolo at its neutral position, allowing easy access to the string lock bolts. It will also make tuning the new strings much easier.

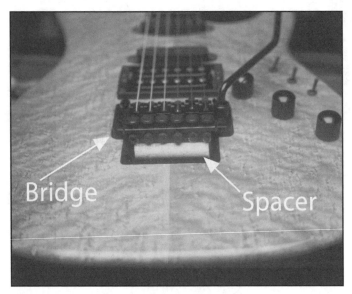

Insert a spacer under the bridge.

Step 2: Loosen nut locks and remove caps.

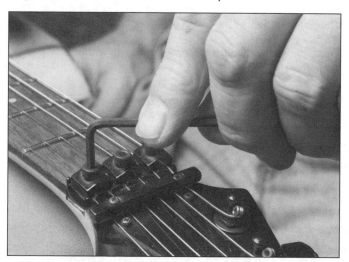

Step 3: De-tune old strings.

Step 4: Loosen string locks.

Step 5: Remove old strings.

Installing New Strings

There are two accepted methods for stringing Floyd Rose tremolos:

Method 1: Insert the string through the tuning machine without removing the ball end.

Method 2: Cut off the ball end just above the over-winding and insert the string into the saddle.

Method 1

Step 1: Insert the plain end of the string through the tuning machine capstan hole and pull it through, bringing the ball end near the capstan.

Step 2: Run the string under the string retainer and over the nut.

Step 3: Pull up any slack until the ball end seats firmly against the tuning machine capstan.

Step 4: Stretch the string past the saddle. Then with wire cutters cut the string even with the back of the saddle.

Step 5: Insert the string between the loosened clamp lock and the saddle.

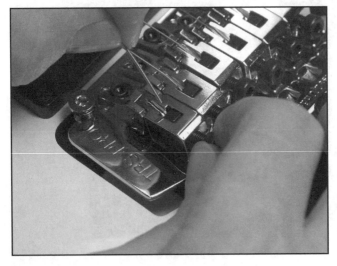

Step 6: Tighten the clamp lock screw.

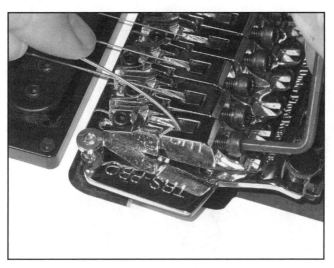

Step 7: Tune to pitch.

Method 2

Step 1: Cut off the ball end just above the over-winding.

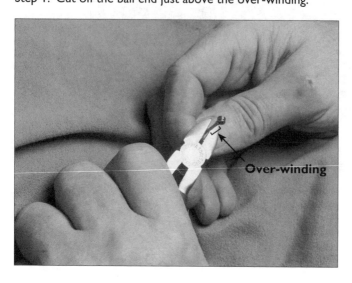

Step 2: Insert the string between the clamp lock and the saddle.

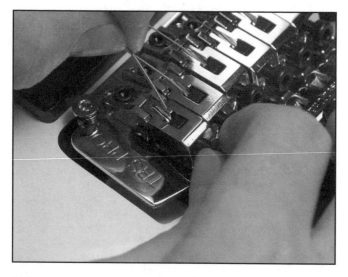

Step 3: Run the string down the neck, over the nut and
under the string retainer.

Step 4: Insert the string through the tuning
machine capstan.

Step 5: Leave about 3–4 inches of slack.

Step 6: Lock the string as shown on the facing page. For "six-in-line" headstocks, lock the strings as for the left side.

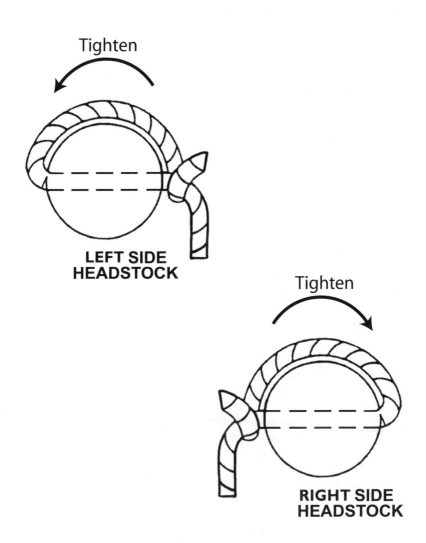

Step 7: Tune to pitch.

After you have completed the restringing, loosen the fine tuners to nearly the full out position.

To stretch each string, pull the string away from the fingerboard about an inch while moving up and down the string. Do this about three or four times to each string. Retune to pitch.

Replace the nut clamps, noting the proper direction (see drawing below). Remove the shim.

Nut Clamps Orientation

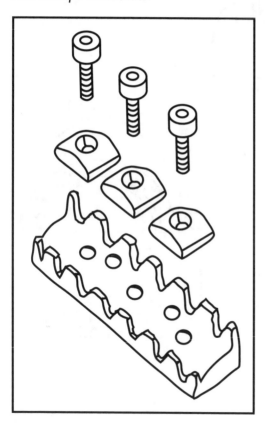

To eliminate problems, there are a couple of basic rules to keep in mind.

1. Make sure that the old broken string ends are removed before installing new ones.

2. Do not over-tighten clamp lock bolts. Over tightening can damage the clamp blocks or the saddle housing.

Also, be aware that:

1. Clamp blocks that have been over-tightened will split and wedge. This will make string insertion very difficult if not impossible.

2. Saddles are susceptible to fracture from over-tightening, and could require costly replacement.

3. Nut lock caps that are over-tightened cause dents in the nut. This can interfere with proper locking.

Adjusting Your Truss Rod

Adjusting the truss rod on a guitar with a Floyd Rose system is the same as the procedure described on pages 22–29.

> **CAUTION**
>
> *Use great care when making truss rod adjustments. Normally, no more than a half turn is required.*

Angle of the Base Plate

After the truss rod has been properly adjusted, it is necessary to adjust the angle of the base plate in relation to the front of the guitar. This is very important because a change in angle can cause a change in action. Normally, the bridge assembly is set parallel to the face of the guitar.

Base plate

This is ideal for two reasons:

1. When making string-length adjustments for intonation, the action will stay the same.

2. You can use this as a visual reference that your guitar is in tune.

Setting the Base Plate Angle

If your base plate isn't parallel to the front of the guitar, it will be necessary to make some adjustments to the spring's tension in the back of your guitar. If the tremolo is tilted away from the front of your guitar, the springs must be tightened.

Conversely, if the tremolo is tilted toward the front of your guitar, the springs must be loosened.

Steps for setting base plate angle:

Step 1: Remove the spring cavity cover, exposing the springs. Note the two adjusting screws on the claw.

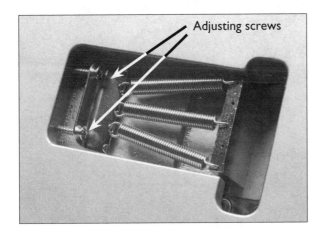

Adjusting screws

Step 2: To increase spring tension, turn the screws in a clockwise direction. To decrease spring tension, turn the screws in a counterclockwise direction. Note that the claw should be parallel to the edge of the cavity in which it sits.

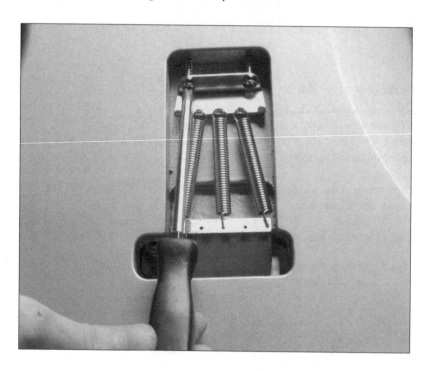

CAUTION

Make adjustments in small increments.

In some cases, it may be necessary to add or remove a spring to achieve the proper balance.

Increases in string gauge require more spring tension, while decreases in string gauge require less spring tension. Make sure that all the springs are matched to each other. Variances in length or tension will interfere with proper operation of the tremolo.

It is very important to retune after each adjustment to properly evaluate the base plate position.

Once the base plate is level and the guitar is tuned to the proper pitch, we can proceed with the action adjustment procedures.

Setting Action at the Bridge

Adjusting the pivot stud on each side of the bridge sets overall action height. Clockwise adjustment lowers the bridge and counter-clockwise raises the bridge.

CAUTION

Some Ibanez pivot posts have internal locking

screws that must be released before

making adjustments, or you may damage

the guitar.

The Procedure

Step 1: With a 6" (or 15 cm) rule, graduated in 64ths, measure the distance from the bottom of the string to the top of the 12th fret (see photo on the next page). This is done on the 1st and 6th strings. Refer to the chart on page 33 for the actual specifications.

Step 2: Adjust the pivot post on the 1st string to specification.

Step 3: Adjust the pivot post on the 6th string to specification.

Step 4: Measure the action of the in-between strings (2nd, 3rd, 4th, and 5th strings).

Step 5: If the action specifications in the chart don't match the measurements that you have taken, it will be necessary to shim the saddles. See page 126 for information about shimming the saddles.

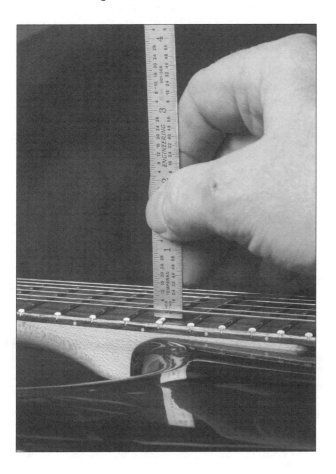

Shimming the Saddles

To gauge the size of the shims that you need, double the difference between the specification and the actual measurement. For example, if you measured the height of the 3rd-string (G) saddle and it was too low by $1/64$", then it would be necessary to put in a shim that is $1/32$" to achieve the right height.

Most Floyd Rose tremolos come with a fixed *radius** (11" or 27.94 cm). This radius is set by having saddles of different height, or by putting steps in the base plate. In some cases, this may not conform to the curvature of the guitar's fingerboard. The easiest way to re-radius the bridge is to place thin metal shims under the saddles.

NOTE

It is a good idea to completely loosen the string before inserting the shims. Also, take note of the position of the saddle in regard to string length, so that you may put it back in the same place as it was. Before moving on to the next saddle, retune the string that was attached to the saddle you just shimmed.

* "Radius" refers to a convex curvature.

In cases where the fingerboard radius (for more on fingerboard radius, see page 188) is less than the bridge's radius, the middle saddles must be shimmed. When the fingerboard radius is greater than the bridge's, the outside saddles must be shimmed. These shims can be purchased from luthier suppliers, guitar repairmen, or you can make your own from shim stock. Shim stock is available from industrial suppliers.

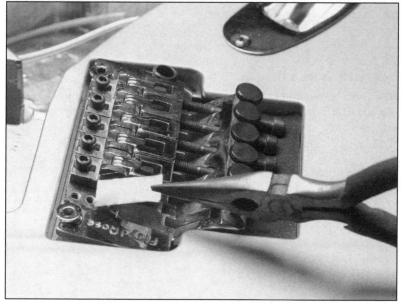

Shimming a saddle.

About the Floyd Rose Nut

Floyd Rose nuts also have a fixed radius. Some manufacturers offer more than one radius, as well as different widths and string spacing. There are some special nuts that are made to accommodate *bullet truss rod* nut adjustments. Introduced in 1966, the bullet truss rod allows Fender-style necks to be adjusted at the headstock—without removing the neck.

Floyd Rose nuts are also available left-handed. On some models, the nut has bolts that go all the way through the neck. On others, the nut is attached from the top by wood screws. There is a photo of a Floyd Rose nut assembly on page 102.

Setting Nut Height

After setting the action at the bridge, the next step is to set the action at the nut. The Floyd Rose nut action is set by putting shims between the nut and the mating surface on the neck.

g the String Retainer

nut has been properly adjusted, the string retainer should also
The string retainer keeps the strings seated in the nut so that
are not sharpened when the nut clamps are locked. The string
s a screw at either end. These screws set the height of the
ner. When the string retainer bar is set properly, the high and
ings should just conform to the top of the nut surface.

Steps for setting the nut height:

1. Using a feeler gauge, measure the space between the first fret
   and the bottom of the string. The normal nut action should be
   .018" or (.04572 cm). If the .018" blade is too tight or too loose,
   use a thinner or thicker blade until you find the size that fits. The
   difference between the two blades will determine the shim size.
   This should be done on the 1st and 6th strings.

2. If your action is lower than spec, you will have to shim the nut. Sometimes, it may be necessary to use different height shims on the bass and treble ends. If your action is too high, you may have to remove some shims. Sometimes, there are no shims to remove. In this case, it will be necessary to remove some wood from under the nut (an experienced technician should do this).

3. After inserting or removing the appropriate shims, be sure to tighten the bolts or screws.

NOTE

In some cases, the curvature of the nut doesn't conform to that of the fingerboard. If the radius of the nut is smaller than that of the fingerboard, it usually doesn't present a problem. If the curvature is greater than that of the fingerboard, the strings in the middle may be too low when the outside strings are normal. This problem can be dealt with in two ways:

1. Get a nut that has the correct radius.

2. Shim the nut higher than normal.

When possible, the best approach is to get a nut. Shimming the nut higher than usual makes playing difficult and aversely affects the intonation.

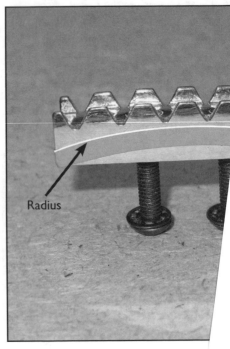

Radius

This is just one possible nut radius.

Setting Intonation (String Length)

The final step in adjusting your Floyd Rose tremolo is to set the intonation. Because of differences in the flexibility of individual strings, it is necessary to set the vibrating length of each string. This will ensure that your guitar will play in tune from note to note and key to key throughout its playing range. Intonation adjustments should be made using an electronic tuner. But if you have a good ear, you may be able to get by.

Steps for setting the intonation:

Step 1: Loosen the nut clamps.

Step 2: Plug your guitar into the electronic tuner and turn it on.

Step 3: Tune all the open strings to the tuner.

Step 4: Start with the 6th (low E) string. Play the harmonic at the 12th fret and then play the fretted octave at the 12th fret. Note if the fretted note is sharp or flat. If the note is flat, the string is too long and must be shortened. Conversely, if the note is sharp, the string must be lengthened.

Step 5: To make the appropriate adjustments without specialized tools, you must loosen the string and unlock the saddle mounting screw.

Step 6: Slide the saddle in the correct direction to compensate for the tuning error: toward the nut to shorten the string, and away from the nut to lengthen it. After a bit of practice, you will be able to judge approximately how much to move the saddles in relation to the amount of error.

Step 7: Relock the saddle screw and retune the string. Check the open 12th fret harmonic against the fretted octave. If they are the same, proceed to the next string. If not, repeat the procedure until they are.

There is a company that makes a tool that clips on to the back of the bridge and the string lock screw, allowing you to make saddle adjustments without detuning. This is very handy and can save a lot of time.

Tremolo Arm Assembly

The older Floyd Rose tremolo had an arm that threaded into a bushing mounted on the base plate. To allow movement of the arm, there was a nylon washer on each side of the base plate. This system had a bad habit of working itself loose. A wrench was needed to remove the arm. Later models featured a new arm design that could be tensioned from the top to control arm movement. This also made it possible to remove the arm with your fingers.

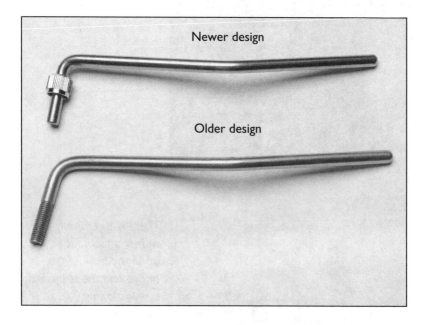

Newer design

Older design

Tools Required for Adjusting Your Floyd Rose Tremolo

A few basic tools are required to adjust the Floyd Rose tremolo.

You will require the following:

1. One Phillips #2 screwdriver (spring claw screws)

2. One straight blade screwdriver (pivot post)

3. One 3 mm Allen wrench (nut and saddle string locks)

4. One 2.5 mm Allen wrench (nut mounting bolts)

5. One 2 mm Allen wrench (saddle lock bolts)

6. One 1.5 mm Allen wrench (pivot stud lock screws for Ibanez models)

7. 6" or 15 cm rule graduated in 64ths or mm (action measurements)

8. One automotive feeler gauge set (nut and truss rod measurements)

9. Two 11 mm open end wrenches (tensioning original style arm)

10. One pair of shears (cutting shim material)

11. One electronic tuner with cord (setting intonation)

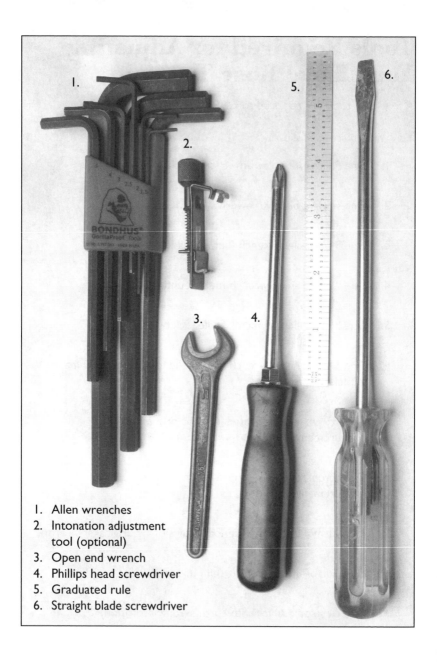

1. Allen wrenches
2. Intonation adjustment
   tool (optional)
3. Open end wrench
4. Phillips head screwdriver
5. Graduated rule
6. Straight blade screwdriver

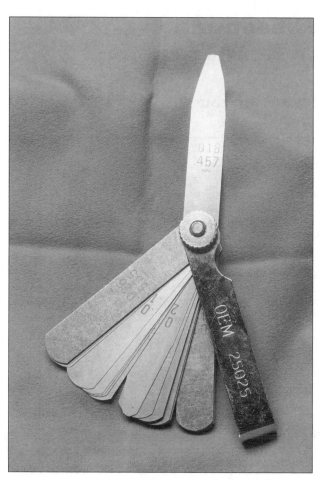

Feeler gauges.

Trouble Shooting
the Floyd Rose Tremolo

Problem: String buzzing

Probable causes:

1. Worn out strings

2. Back bowed neck

3. Pickups set too high

4. Wear in the nut or saddle

5. Fret buzz

6. Strings not clamped properly

7. Defective casting on the nut or saddle

Solutions:

1. Examine the strings for wear or corrosion. Replace if necessary. Re-check for buzz.

2. Check truss rod adjustment. Reset if necessary.

3. Fret the string at the last fret. Visually inspect the space between the pickup and the string. Lower if necessary.

4. Inspect the area where the string contacts the nut and saddle. If wear marks or corrosion are present, replace the part.

5. Examine the frets for wear. Observe if the buzzing only occurs in a specific area. Dress and re-round or replace the frets (for more on fret maintenance, see page 194).

6. The string should be clamped in the middle of the nut and saddle slots. To determine if you have a nut or saddle buzz, fret the string at the first fret. If the buzz stops, the buzz is at the nut.

7. Replace the defective part.

Problem: Excessive string breakage

Solution:

1. Replace worn-out strings.

2. Avoid over-tightening the string clamp at the nut.

3. Excessive string breakage can be caused by corrosion at the string contact point of the nut or saddle. Replace worn or corroded parts.

Problem: Tremolo can't be adjusted to sit parallel to the face of the guitar with claw adjustment all the way in

Solution:

1. The string gauge may be excessive for the amount of springs counteracting the force. Add more springs as needed.

2. The springs may have been over-extended causing them to be damaged. If this is the case, they should be replaced.

Remember: The springs should match each other.

Problem: The guitar won't stay in tune

Solution:

1. The strings need to be stretched.

2. Check to see if nut clamps are properly locked.

3. Check for grooves in the nut and nut clamps. Replace if necessary.

4. Check nut-mounting bolts for tightness.

5. Check intonation adjustments.

6. Check for loose neck screws.

7. Check springs for mismatch or contact with the body or back plate.

8. Check pivot studs and knife-edges for excess wear.

9. Check for loose pivot studs or misalignment.

10. Check for magnetic pull from the pickups. Lower pickups.

Problem: Fine tuners won't adjust

Solution:

1. Saddle pivot points corroded. Lubricate.

Problem: Height adjustment screws are bottomed out, but the action is still too high

Solution:

1. This problem is caused by insufficient neck angle. It can be remedied by removing the neck and placing a shim in between the neck pocket and the heel of the neck.

2. One other solution is to cut a recess in the front of the guitar provided that it doesn't already have one.

Problem: When I use my tremolo, the springs make noise

Solution:

1. Coat the springs with silicon RTV.

2. Lubricate the spring attachment points.

Helpful Hint

Some players would rather have tuning stability than be able to pull up on their tremolo. This can accomplished by blocking the tremolo so that the arm works only in the down mode.

Steps:

1. Make a block of wood just thick enough to fit between the sustain block and the edge of the spring cavity when the tremolo is in the rest position. Glue a thin layer of felt or hard rubber on the side of the block facing the sustain block. This will eliminate body noise when the tremolo returns to the neutral position.

2. Glue the block of wood in place between the sustain block and the edge of the spring cavity.

3. Tighten the claw adjustment screws, until you can bend notes without the tremolo pulling away from the body.

This modification will keep the guitar in tune even if a string should break. It is also useful for players who bend notes against pedal tones.

PART 2: GEAR ESSENTIALS

Strings

Strings can make or break any guitar. If you let them get too old, fretted notes can end up sounding a half step, or more, flat. Buzzing and other problematic sounds can often be fixed simply by changing the strings. Assuming that you have fresh strings, it still makes a huge difference which kind you use. For instance, you'll never sound like Charlie Christian with light-gauge strings, and you'll never sound like Eddie Van Halen with heavy ones. Let's discuss several aspects of the string itself to better understand the situation.

Gauge

String *gauge* (thickness) is measured in thousandths of an inch, and sets of guitar strings are often referred to by the measurement of the high-E string. For instance, if the 1st string (high-E string) in a set of guitar strings is 0.009", then the set is referred to as a 9-gauge set or, simply, a set of 9s. Most electric guitars come from the factory strung with 9s. This generally means the six strings are the following gauges:

1st String	2nd String	3rd String
.009"	.011"	.016"
4th String	5th String	6th String
.024"	.032"	.042"

A 9-gauge set of guitar strings may be called "light" or "super slinky," depending on the manufacturer. On the next page is a table showing the most common electric guitar string set gauges.

1st String	2nd String	3rd String
.008"	.011"	.014"
.009"	.011"	.016"
.010"	.013"	.017"
.011"	.014"	.018"
.012"	.016"	.020"
.013"	.017"	.026"
4th String	5th String	6th String
.022"	.030"	.038"
.024"	.032"	.042"
.026"	.036"	.046"
.028"	.038"	.048"
.032"	.042"	.054"
.036"	.046"	.056"

The table above doesn't reflect every string-gauge combination. Manufacturers also offer "hybrid" sets that combine the first three strings from one set with the last three of an adjacent one, so for example the high strings of a 9-gauge set are combined with the low strings of a 10-gauge set. This creates a "light top, heavy bottom" effect. The idea is to create a string set that offers a beefy low-end sound but also facilitates easy string bending.

String gauge affects playability and tone. The lighter the string, the easier it is to press down and to bend, but the overall sound will also be thinner. It makes sense that the fatter the string, the fatter the tone; listen to Stevie Ray Vaughan, who used 13-gauge strings, for a perfect example. Eric Clapton and George Harrison used light-gauge strings as they were interested in bending more easily and didn't mind the trade-off in tone. Many players who use heavy strings opt to tune down a half step, which will decrease string tension, making it easier to bend and leading to a much fatter sound.

Stevie Ray Vaughan (1954–1990) used 13-gauge strings, as evidenced by his fat tone. Others players, like Eric Clapton and George Harrison, used light-gauge strings, as they were interested in bending more easily and didn't mind the trade-off in tone.

Types of String Windings

Roundwound

On a typical set of electric guitar strings, the 1st, 2nd, and 3rd strings are unwound, while the rest are wound. In some heavier-gauge sets, the 3rd string will also be wound. In most cases, the core wire is round with another round wire wrapped around it. This is called a *roundwound* string and is used by most rock, pop, and blues players. The exterior round wire that wraps around the core string creates a bit of texture on the surface of the string, resulting in a bright sound that produces some string rasp while sliding (of course, this works really well for pick slides).

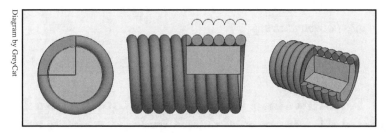

Diagram of a roundwound string.

Flatwound

Another type of winding is called *flatwound,* where the exterior winding is done with a flat wire instead of a round one. Flatwounds are preferred by jazz players because they reduce string rasp and result in a comparatively "dead" sound. The player's finger glides more easily across the string's smooth surface on flatwound strings.

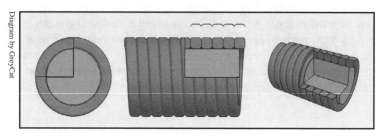

Diagram of a flatwound string.

Half Roundwound and Quarter Roundwound

There are several varieties of partially flattened wrapping wires, including *half roundwound* and *quarter roundwound* strings. These feature shallower crevices in between the wrappings, bridging the gap between round and flatwound strings to give players more options to choose from.

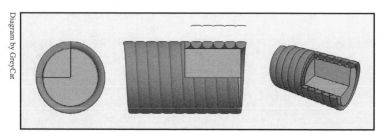

Diagram of half roundwound string.

Materials

Ernie Ball's "Regular Slinky" electric guitar strings feature a nickel-plated steel wire wrapped around a tin-plated, hex-shaped steel core wire. The tin plating helps fight corrosion, which will easily shorten the life of guitar strings. Ernie Ball's practice of using hex-shaped core wires is somewhat unusual though. The core wire most commonly used by string manufacturers, including D'Addario, Dean Markley, and DR, is a round, solid steel wire. The wrapping is most commonly nickel-plated steel, or in some cases pure nickel. Though, hexagonal core wire is also offered by D'Addario, among others, in select packs. Ernie Ball also makes strings that feature a solid steel core wrapped with a unique iron/cobalt alloy. Cobalt players claim the strings offer better sustain and punch, and last longer.

Ball End

The ball end of a string makes a huge difference in quality, mostly because that's where a string usually breaks. Therefore, the method of attachment is very important. Bargain strings tend to have poorly attached ends that break quite easily. Of course, major brands generally do a better job of attaching the ends, leading to longer-lasting strings.

In addition, the ball end may differ from one string manufacturer to another. Ernie Ball offers the option of reinforced ball ends for longer string life. D'Addario color codes the ends of their strings for easier identification since their eco-friendly packaging doesn't individually wrap each string. Fender offers a "bullet" end, which is heavier and larger, to create more sustain, Fender claims.

Coated Strings

String coating is a relatively recent development. Elixir was the first company to manufacture coated strings, and by 2000 they had swept the market. Elixir's process involves coating the string with a thin, evenly applied insulating plastic-like substance. The coating seals the string, preventing moisture, such as sweat and skin oil, to set in and corrode the string. Depending on the string manufacturer, the various materials used to coat strings include polymers and Teflon-like materials. With the extra materials involved in manufacturing, coated strings are usually priced a bit higher than conventional strings. And, bear in mind, only the wound strings are usually coated.

As we all know, the rusted string is a tone-destroying abomination that must be avoided. So, the coated string is obviously the answer, right? They certainly do last longer, which is why so many acoustic guitars come strung with them straight from the factory even though they are a little more expensive. Since the gaps on the string surface created in the wrapping process are partially filled by the coating, string rasp and fret wear are reduced. But when the string begins to wear out, little shards of the coating material will start to dangle off the string. This may not be quite as bad as rust, but it's fairly annoying.

There are other factors to consider with coated strings. The strings will feel a little slippery and impart a slightly different tone. It's hard to pin down the difference, but the resulting tone change seems to lend itself better to acoustic than to electric playing. Electric guitarists might consider just buying less expensive conventional strings and changing them more frequently.

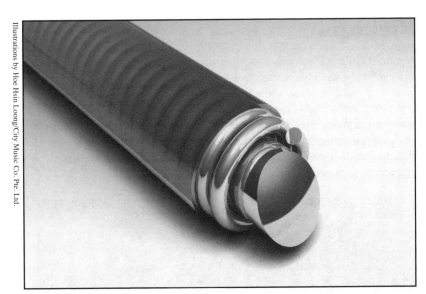

Coated wound string.

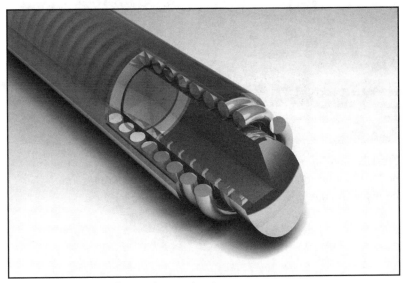

Cross-section view of coated wound string.

Pickups

A guitar *pickup* is essentially a magnet with six metal pole pieces wrapped in wire. There have been many design variations, such as additional pole pieces, multiple magnets, additional winding, onboard battery amplification, and more, but the basic design and concept has remained the same through the years. The vibrations of a guitar string pass through a magnetic field and are converted into electronic signals that are then sent to an amplifier through an instrument cable. Pickups come in three basic categories: single-coil, humbucking, and active.

Photo by Jan Krömer

The vibrations of a guitar string pass through a magnetic field (above) and are converted into electronic signals that are then sent to an amplifier through an instrument cable (see next page).

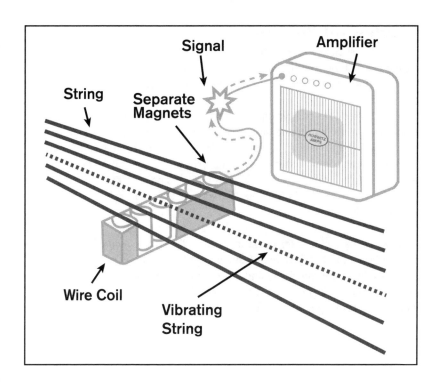

Single-Coil Pickups

The *single-coil* pickup is the original electric guitar pickup. George Beauchamp pioneered this design in the mid-1920s while moving toward creating the first solid-body electric guitar, the "Frying Pan."

The average single-coil pickup produces a relatively low volume output signal with a fair amount of hum in it. If a guitarist is using clean or low-gain tones, then this isn't a problem. Think clean funk, blues, and rock rhythm guitar tones. Listen to Jimi Hendrix's intro to "Little Wing" for an example of the sound. Additional well-known single-coil players include Charlie Christian, David Gilmour, Stevie Ray Vaughan, Eric Clapton, and Yngwie Malmsteen.

Today's single-coil pickups range from the full, warm sound of the Gibson-style P-90 to the buzzy chime of the vintage Strat-style version. The single-coil tone has a certain clarity and purity that is unmatched by any other pickup. Modern single-coils are also available in noiseless quiet models that function beautifully in high-gain situations.

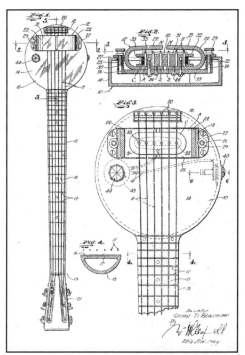

Diagram of Beauchamp's "Frying Pan" lap steel guitar from his 1934 patent application.

Photo by David Monniaux

Modern single-coil pickups.

Humbucking Pickups

Humbucking pickups, also called double-coil pickups or simply humbuckers, are commonly found on Gibson-style and other electric guitars that are designed to produce louder, darker, and potentially higher-gain sounds. The humbucker uses two coils to "buck the hum" (or cancel out the interference), induced by the alternating current in single-coil pickups; the resulting humbucker is louder and considerably less noisy than single-coil pickups. The humbucking sound can be used for anything from clean, fat jazz tones to classic rock and heavy metal.

Open-coil (uncovered) humbucking pickups.

Covered humbuckers.

Humbucker devotees include Joe Pass, George Benson, Les Paul, B. B. King, Jimmy Page, Frank Zappa, Slash, Eddie Van Halen, and many others. Listen to the intro to "Sweet Child o' Mine" by Guns N' Roses for an example of the humbucker distortion sound.

Active Pickups

Active pickups are battery-powered electromagnetic pickups that amplify a guitar's signal to send out a higher gain signal to the amplifier. They come in many varieties, including some that feature active equalizers or filters for extra tone shaping. Active pickups have several advantages, compared to other pickups: they are virtually noiseless, have better sustain, and the tone doesn't change when you turn the volume down. Since they are about 95% less magnetic than regular pickups, they never generate unpleasant tones by being set too close to the strings, nor are they susceptible to noise generated by being close to light fixtures—as you would find with non-active pickups, also known as *passive* pickups. EMG is the most popular brand for active pickups. The convenient thing with EMGs is once a guitar is wired for them, they can easily be switched to other EMG pickups without having to solder wires.

Most modern bass guitars have active pickups as do most acoustic-electric guitars. Heavy metal guitarists tend to prefer active pickups because they deliver more distortion, therefore 7- and 8-string guitars often come standard with active pickups.

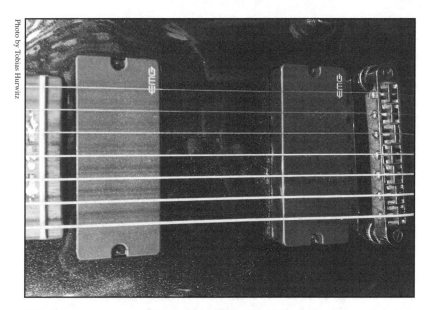

7-String Schecter Diamond Series with active EMG Pickups.

When an instrument cable is plugged into the output jack of a guitar equipped with active pickups, the 9-volt battery onboard is always running, whether or not the guitar is being played. So, it's important to remember to unplug your guitar when you're not playing. The 9-volt battery onboard should last from six months to a year, unless it is drained prematurely by keeping the cable plugged in.

It seems like active pickups have many benefits, so why doesn't everyone use them? There could be a few reasons. First, high-profile active pickup users, like David Gilmour and Metallica, attract a lot of attention and might influence many players to get into active pickups. But, players of their stature have guitar techs who handle the maintenance of constantly changing batteries. It's easy for the high-profile guitarists to enjoy the benefits without the hassles. The average kid who buys a bass with an active pickup installed is another story. He might not even know it needs batteries until his tone has gradually degenerated into an anemic, noisy, distorted mess. Then, it completely cuts out.

Then there's the higher output situation. Though a small percentage of active pickups deliver moderate output levels, these are few and far between. Guitar amps, pedals, and processors react very differently to varying amounts of input gain. Frankly, they're usually designed to function normally and correctly with the signal of a passive pickup. A passive single-coil pickup yields a crystal-clear tone and a passive bridge-position humbucker might just start to break up, but an active pickup would almost certainly overdrive an amp. It may be difficult to get a crystal-clear, undistorted tone from an active pickup without turning the volume knob down slightly on the guitar.

Handwound Pickups

Even in the old days of pickup manufacturing, circa the 1950s, pickups weren't wrapped by hand, so the term "handwound" may be a little misleading. To make a pickup, an operator would guide a wire into place as the machine wrapped it around the magnet; there are generally between 5,000 to 10,000 wraps of hair-thin copper wire. This slightly unpredictable process created pickups that were anything but consistent. Varying degrees of tightness or looseness in the coil, differing numbers of wraps per coil, crossed wires, and other anomalies were involved in the making of pickups of the same make, model, and year. The resulting pickups could sound freakishly great, though were often just average and even subpar. Consistency was not a hallmark of pickup manufacturing in the old days.

Modern manufacturing techniques allow for consistent pickup winding, which means all of the pickups for a particular make, model, and year will sound virtually identical. Improved performance can be systematically engineered instead of being happened upon by chance. Nonetheless, many players still swear by handwound pickups. They are definitely unique, and if you get a good one, no one else will have exactly the same tone as you!

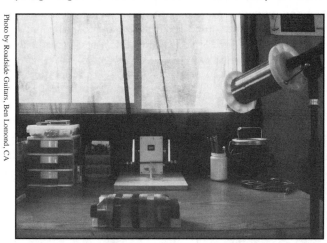

Pickup-winding station.

New coil winding on a Jackson pickup.

Electronics

Guitar electronics can range from the very simple single humbucker, single volume knob approach championed by Eddie Van Halen on his infamous "Frankenstein" guitar to the marvelously complex controls and active preamps on a 1970s B.C. Rich Bich guitar. Most players and manufacturers choose something more moderate, with the two classic setups being that of the Fender Stratocaster and the Gibson Les Paul. Of course, many other options are available. Paul Reed Smith, Gibson, B.C. Rich, and others offer five-position rotary knobs, tone switches, phase inverters, coil taps, kill switches, active preamps, and more. We're going to explore the two classic setups first.

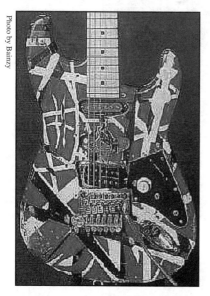

Photo by Bainzy

The Eddie Van Halen "Frankenstein" guitar has minimal electronics.

Photo by Coyle182

The Tom Delonge Signature ES-335 has minimal electronics.

Jerry Garcia "Rosebud" guitar with complex electronics.

B.C. Rich Bich 10-string guitar features two active-boost circuits with individual controls.

Fender Stratocaster Setup

The classic Stratocaster features a versatile and intelligent electronic design with a layout that allows for quite a few tonal variations. For one thing, the single-coil pickups can be combined in adjacent pairs to create a humbucking-type sound. The resulting sound from combining the single-coils isn't quite as beefy as a real humbucker, but the hum is definitely eliminated! By flipping the pickup selector switch to the setting closest to the ground, you activate the bridge pickup to get the brashest sound available. There are countless subtle variations available with different pickup, tone knob, and volume knob combinations.

The classic Fender Stratocaster features three single-coil pickups, a five-position blade switch, one volume, and two tone controls.

Stratocaster Blade Switch Function

Position 1: (all the way up) Neck pickup only

Position 2: Combines neck and middle pickups

Position 3: Middle pickup only

Position 4: Combines middle and bridge pickups

Position 5: Bridge pickup only

Knob Functions

Volume: Works on all pickups and combinations.

Tone 1: Works on neck pickup only

Tone 2: Works on middle pickup only

The Strat has evolved to include many new and improved options over the years. It all began with the trend toward so-called "Superstrats," which were modified Strats that featured a humbucker in the bridge position. This was a major improvement because it allowed the Strat to enter sonic territory previously reserved for Gibson and its imitators.

Today, an American-made Deluxe Fender Stratocaster features powerful and improved controls. It looks exactly like the classic Strat layout, which is part of the charm. On today's Deluxe Strat, the pickups are all noiseless—so quiet their performance rivals that of traditional humbuckers. Also, there is an additional pickup concealed under the pickguard, which is activated by pressing a button in the volume knob. When engaged, it turns any of the five positions into a true humbucker!

Gibson Les Paul Setup

The Gibson Les Paul features an equally intelligent and versatile set of controls that are completely different from the Fender Strat. The Gibson features two humbucking pickups and a three-way toggle switch that selects either one pickup or combines both. Each pickup has its own dedicated volume and tone control. The creamy, warm neck pickup, the airy and harmonically rich middle position, and the aggressive bridge position humbucker all provide solid and usable sounds.

The Les Paul's simple three-way toggle switch configuration allows for a type of channel-switching function onboard the guitar. This is particularly useful for players who favor the "straight amping" approach where a guitar is plugged straight into an amp with no pedals or additional effects. To achieve channel-switching onboard a Gibson-style guitar, simply turn the volume and tone down a bit on the neck pickup while leaving the bridge pickup controls full up. With a little gain dialed in on the amp, you'll have a clean, warm sound with your toggle switch at the neck pickup position and a louder, brighter distorted tone with it down at the bridge position. In the middle, you'll split the difference in tone. Feel free to tweak and balance the contrast on the two pickups to your liking.

Gibson Les Paul Standard.

A variation on the channel-switching idea is the "kill-switch" effect, which has been used by Tom Morello, Buckethead, Randy Rhoads, and others. To get this effect, simply turn the volume and tone controls all the way down on one of the pickups while leaving the controls for the other pickup full up—this way, your toggle switch will function as a kill switch. Toggling back and forth between pickups will result in an on-and-off sound. This is very useful with distortion. Try it!

Series and Parallel Pickup Wiring

A humbucking pickup can be wired in *series* or *parallel*. Typically, pickup wiring is done in series, which means the output of one coil is run through the other, and a single output is created by combining the outputs of both coils. In parallel wiring, each coil of the humbucker has a separate output which is combined later in the circuit. The sound is a little fatter with series wiring, which is why guitars often come this way from the factory.

Single-coil pickups are usually wired parallel, but in series wiring, the resulting sound has a humbucking quality. It doesn't sound exactly like a true humbucker, because the coils aren't right next to each other, but the combined pickups buck the hum even if they lack the muscle of a real humbucker. When positions 2 or 4 of the five-position blade switch are activated on a Strat, parallel wiring of single-coil pickups is engaged (unless they are wired to achieve something different). Those settings buck the hum but create a "quacky" sound due to the fact that pairs of adjacent pickups are *out of phase* with one another. Sound waves that are in phase with each other have peaks and valleys that are perfectly aligned so that the sound is strengthened. Out of phase waves are unsynchronized so that the peaks and valleys don't line up. If two waves are exactly out of phase they may cancel each other out, completely silencing the wave. This phenomenon is called *phase cancellation*. The waves of two adjacent pickups are partially out of phase and when combined create an interesting and desirable tone. Eric Clapton and other players of older Strats with three-position blade switches used to wedge the blade halfway between positions to get this sound.

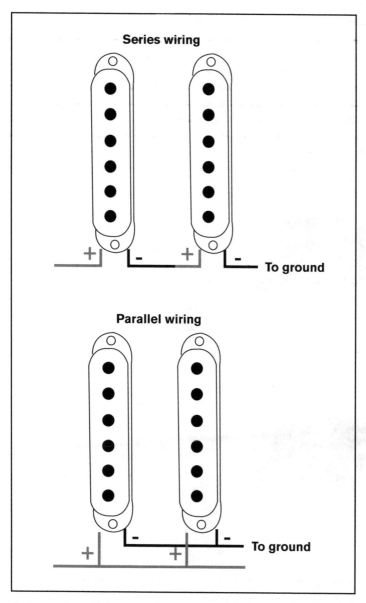

Series and parallel wiring of single-coil pickups.

Coil Tapping and Splitting

Coil *splitting* is often mistakenly referred to as coil *tapping.* Coil splitting disengages one of the two pickups inside a humbucker so that it sounds like a single coil. It is often activated by a push-pull potentiometer (that is doubling as the volume or tone knob) or via a simple mini toggle switch. This is a common modification that will come stock on many guitars. As Strat players load their guitars with humbuckers and add kill switches to make them more versatile, Les Paul players will add coil splitting to get closer to the clean Strat tones.

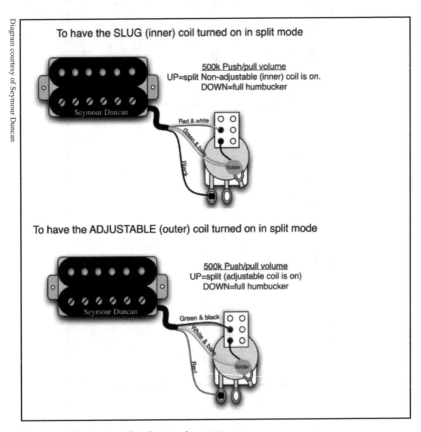

Seymour Duncan coil splitting diagram.

Coil tapping is quite different. Here, a portion of a single-coil pickup, often the bridge position, is tapped into to slightly color the overall sound, making it quieter, clearer, yet purely Stratty in a good way. Switching from the tapped pickup to the full-on one with a little gain on the amp can take you from crystal clean to mean in a heartbeat! This cool procedure is mostly overlooked; people who refer to coil tapping are often talking about coil splitting.

Custom staggered SSL-5 with tapped version available for dual output levels.

In and Out of Phase

A phase-inverting toggle switch can deliver more options as you combine pickups. When two wave forms are synchronized, so that the peak of each wave reaches the same amplitude (volume) at the same time, the waves are in phase. If the opposite is the case, so that the valley of one wave happens just when the other wave is peaking, then they are out of phase. Waves that are in phase get twice as loud and ones that are exactly out of phase cancel each other out completely, resulting in total silence.

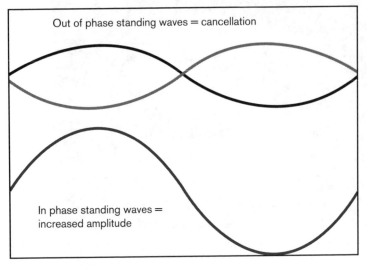

Out of phase standing waves = cancellation

In phase standing waves = increased amplitude

In and out of phase.

If a phase toggle switch is wired into a single-coil pickup, you will hear no difference at all when the switch is engaged, unless there is another pickup being used at the same time. When there are two pickups, the engagement of the switch changes the interaction of the waves being generated by the two pickups from being in phase, which creates a louder sound, to being out of phase, which partially cancels the signals so that certain frequencies are eliminated. A weaker, "quacky" sound results. Total phase cancellation doesn't occur when the switch is engaged because the pickups are not exact duplicates and are mounted in different locations. Therefore, they don't create identical waves or exhibit complete phase cancellation.

Kill Switches

A fairly common electronic modification is the addition of a kill switch to a Strat-style guitar or any guitar that can't get the same effect with stock electronics. Tom Morello and Buckethead both did this mod but in completely different ways. The toggle switch used by Morello activates the guitar when the switch is thrown down, so that when he hammers down onto a note it pops on and both hands work in unison. This would be absolutely counterintuitive with the arcade-style push button switch used by Buckethead. The Buckethead switch kills the guitar signal when it is pushed down. Try to play a Rage Against the Machine lick with this type of switch, and you'll drive yourself crazy! Eddie Van Halen can be heard using a kill switch at the end of his solo on "You Really Got Me" from Van Halen's debut, and Randy Rhoads can be heard using one on the rhythm guitar part to "I Don't Know" from *Blizzard of Ozz*.

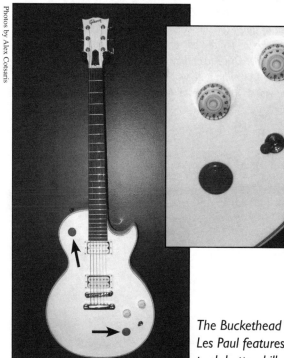

Close-up of push-button kill switch.

The Buckethead signature model Les Paul features two large, red push-button kill switches.

Tone Woods

A tone wood is a wood that produces an actual pitch when a block of it is properly dried and then struck with an object such as a small mallet or drumstick. Plywood doesn't really qualify because the grains running in different directions hamper the natural resonance of the wood. That's why it's always best to choose an acoustic guitar made with as much solid wood as possible, especially the top. If the top isn't made of solid wood, it can't resonate well enough to project the best quality tone.

Acoustic Note: *The wood on an acoustic guitar is much more important to tone than it is on an electric guitar, because the acoustic guitar must stand alone without electronics or amplification. The sound of an acoustic guitar depends wholly on wood, strings, craftsmanship, and design. Even so, the importance of wood quality has been questioned by some notable luthiers. The "Pallet Guitar," from Taylor Guitars, makes a case for the importance of design and craftsmanship over the use of fancy tone woods. Taylor recycled wood from actual shipping pallets to make 25 limited edition guitars. The guitars sound remarkably good and play easily! Of course, they probably would have sounded better if they had been made from fine tone woods, but the point is made: even on an acoustic guitar, tone wood isn't the be all and end all.*

Taylor "Pallet Guitar."

Plywood in Electric Guitars

In electric guitar construction, tone wood is less important than in acoustic guitar construction. This is because electric guitar tone comes mainly from the pickups and strings. Many solid-body electrics will feature plywood bodies that are sanded down and painted brightly. These guitars are played on stages worldwide without having noticeably inferior tone. Expensive and highly regarded archtops, like the Gibson ES-335, also have plywood tops.

Photo by Tobias Hurwitz

Cheap plywood-body electric guitar (Fender Squier).

Expensive plywood-top electric guitar (Gibson ES-335).

The luthier who is concerned with creating a high-quality instrument, not just a cheap one, will try to build an electric guitar that sounds as good as possible unplugged. The theory is if it sounds good unplugged, then it'll sound even better plugged in, which is probably true. Tone woods do sound better than plywood, and it does, in fact, make a difference. The neck and body both affect the sound, and these can be made with single-wood or multi-wood construction. Tone woods sound, look, and feel different from each other, and some are endangered species, making them extremely difficult to obtain. Luthiers have been known to "harvest" antique desks to get their hands on small quantities of guitar-grade Brazilian rosewood—a highly desirable tone wood. Many consumers just want to see a stunning flamed maple top peeking through a translucent finish on their guitar, and some like the smooth tight-grained feel of an ebony fingerboard under their fingers. These, and many other factors, come into play when building or choosing a guitar.

Let's have a look at a few guitars and the woods used to construct them.

Wood Setup for Gibson SG Standard

Body: Mahogany
Neck: Mahogany
Fingerboard: Indian Rosewood

Photo courtesy of Gibson USA

Gibson SG Standard.

Mahogany

The Les Paul Special, Les Paul Jr., and the SG all have bodies and necks made from mahogany, which has a warm, dark tone with a pleasant but subdued high end, along with good sustain, grit, and character. The color of mahogany is medium to dark brown with a cross grain that makes it a very stable wood. It comes mainly from Africa and Central America, and is often combined with other fine tone woods, such as maple, to form multi-wood bodies like those on the Paul Reed Smith Custom 24 and Gibson Les Paul.

Indian Rosewood

Indian rosewood is the most commonly used wood for modern fingerboard construction in electric guitars. The color is a darker brown than mahogany, and the grain is somewhat loose, imparting a feeling of slight grit or resistance when bending or sliding, unlike the smoother feel of maple, ebony, and Brazilian rosewood fingerboards. The tone is dark as well. Leo Fender introduced rosewood fingerboards as a substitution for maple ones in 1959. Fender had teetered back and forth as to which to use over the years until both were finally offered as options.

Brazilian Rosewood

Brazilian rosewood is a rare and endangered wood. It's heavier than Indian rosewood and offers superior tone and smoother feel. Brazilian rosewood is used for many purposes including the back and sides of acoustic guitars, necks, fingerboards, and more.

Wood Setup for Paul Reed Smith Custom 24

Body: Mahogany with carved flame maple top
Neck: Mahogany
Fingerboard: Indian Rosewood

Photo by Tobias Hurwitz

*Paul Reed Smith
Custom 24.*

Maple

There are several varieties of maple, each with lovely but differing grain
patterns. The flamed, quilted, and bird's eye varieties of maple are often seen
shining through translucent or sunburst finishes on guitars with carved tops.
This creates not only a stunning visual effect, but an enhancement in tone
and comfort. Maple is lighter in weight and brighter in tone than mahogany,
so when a carved maple top is attached to a mahogany body, the finished
guitar is lighter, better sounding, and fancier looking.

Maple is also used for fingerboards and guitar necks. Maple fingerboards
are smooth and produce snappy, bright tones.

Wood Setup for Fender Stratocaster

Body: Swamp Ash
Neck: Maple
Fingerboard: Maple

Fender Stratocaster.

Swamp Ash

The bodies of classic 1950s-era Fender guitars were made of swamp ash, a wood that is still commonly used for the bodies of fine guitars. This dark-blond wood looks great under a translucent finish and is known for its sweet twang. Guitar-grade swamp ash must be taken from the lower part of the tree, which is often submerged in water. It grows in the wetlands of the southern United States and is light and resonant. Northern ash is harder and offers more brightness but isn't generally preferred over swamp ash, which is considered the best ash for guitar building.

Wood Setup for Carvin Custom 7-String

Body: Koa
Neck: Koa with maple stripes
Fingerboard: Ebony

Carvin Custom 7-String.

Koa

Koa is an exotic reddish-brown wood that is only found in the Hawaiian Islands. Though fast growing, Koa is a protected wood so it isn't used much for mass-produced guitars. It is more likely to be found in limited editions and as an option when custom ordering a high-end guitar. Koa delivers a warm, balanced tone with a distinctive upper midrange.

Ebony

Ebony is the hardest wood available for guitar construction and is very expensive and desirable. The grain is very tight, making it almost invisible, and the surface is smooth, which is an ideal match for fast playing when used as a fingerboard wood. The hardness of the wood makes for a durable fingerboard, less susceptible to denting and firmly holding the frets in place. The tone is clear and bright with nice string attack, and the dark, black color makes it visually attractive.

More About Guitar-Building Materials

Dozens of types of woods, exotic and otherwise, have been used in guitar construction, but synthetic materials, such as Plexiglass, resin, and metal, have been used as well. The choices are many and the materials used will affect tone, feel, and appearance.

The words used to describe the sonic properties of wood are subjective at best. Who can say exactly what gritty, full, resonant, brilliant, snappy, murky, chimey, or balanced really means in terms of the subtle differences heard in the resonant frequencies of planks or chunks of lumber? Even wood cut from the same tree, then dried or finished differently, will sound different. The understanding of tone woods is a deep and complex topic that will forever spark innovation and debate among luthiers and guitar enthusiasts. Hopefully, this brief discussion has helped clarify some of the varieties and variables available for consideration.

Fingerboard Radius

Though the fingerboard of a guitar may appear flat at first glance, it is actually curved. As mentioned earlier, this curvature, measured at the nut, is called the fingerboard radius. Manufacturers describe fingerboard radius as a measurement in inches. The smaller the measurement, which represents the size of the circle, the greater the curvature of the fingerboard. This may seem counterintuitive, but understand that the measurement refers to the radius of a circle. See the diagram below for a clearer representation of the concept.

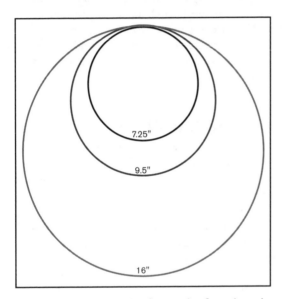

The larger the circle, the flatter the fingerboard.

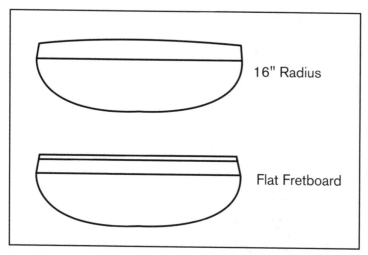

The 16" radius is typical of a Jackson-style guitar whereas the flat fingerboard is found on a nylon-string classical guitar.

How Radius Affects Playability and Performance

Rhythm guitarists tend to like guitars with more curvature in the fingerboard because it makes playing barre chords and chord-melodies easier. The downside to more curvature is it makes bending notes and playing scales slightly more difficult. For this reason, lead guitarists and sweep pickers tend to choose guitars with flatter fingerboards. There are certainly exceptions to this trend, and the difference in playability is subtle enough that most of us can easily switch from a vintage Stratocaster, with a highly curved fingerboard, to a classical guitar, with a perfectly flat one, with little or no difficulty.

Compound or Conical Fingerboard Radius

Some luthiers have attempted to create a best-of-both-worlds scenario by crafting fingerboards with a diminishing radius. The lower part is curved more to make rhythm playing easier, while the high part is flatter to facilitate bending and scale runs. The radius for these guitars changes smoothly since it is modeled on a cone, not a circle. The diagrams below illustrate this concept.

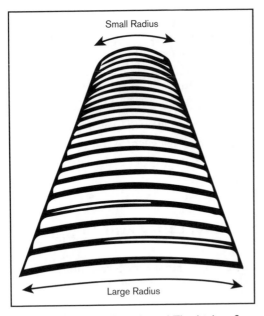

Compound radius fingerboard. The higher frets are less curved than the lower frets.

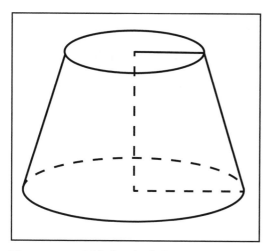

The cone model helps the luthier achieve a smooth radius change because the circles evenly diminish in size as they rise up the cone.

The following chart shows the fingerboard radius of various guitars.

Guitar Neck Radius Guide

GUITAR	RADIUS
Classical Guitar	Flat
Vintage Fender Strat	7.25"
Modern Fender Strat	9.5"
PRS Custom 24	11.5"
Guitars with Original Floyd Rose Locking Nut	10"
Gibson Guitars	10" to 12"
Ibanez Guitars	12"
Jackson Guitars	16"

Scale Length

Scale length is the length of the guitar string from the nut to the bridge—the vibrating portion of the string. It's calculated by measuring from the edge of the nut, where it meets the fingerboard, to the center of the 12th fret and then doubling that distance.

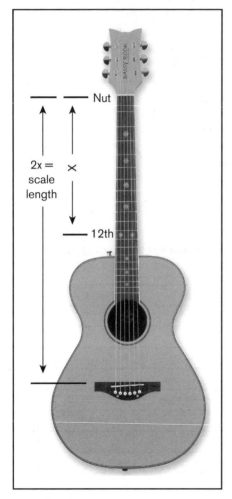

Scale length.

The reason scale length is not simply calculated by measuring from the nut to the bridge is because bridges and bridge saddles are almost always set at an angle to achieve proper intonation. This variation of string length is called *compensation*. If you've ever set the intonation on a guitar with an adjustable bridge you've noticed that the string saddles tend to line up in angled rows of three saddles. This pattern is common to all makes and models of electric guitars with adjustable bridge saddles, but the angle makes measuring from nut to bridge iffy at best, so that's why it's best to determine scale length by measuring from the nut to the center of the 12th fret and then doubling.

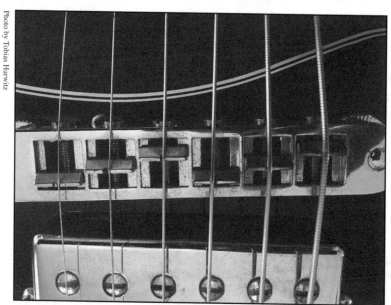

Photo by Tobias Hurwitz

Note the two angled rows of saddles on this properly adjusted bridge.

Conventional Scale Lengths

Many guitars are modeled after the scale length of Fender Stratocasters and Telecasters, which is 25.5". Gibson and Gibson-style guitars tend to feature a shorter scale length of 24.75" with slight variations. Paul Reed Smith guitars fall just between the two at an even 25". This small difference in length of only 0.75" or so can substantially affect the tone and feel of guitars.

The two most-immediately tangible qualities affected by scale length are string tension and harmonic response. The slightly shorter scale length of a Gibson-style guitar produces less string tension, which makes bending strings and pressing down a bit easier than it would be on the longer Fender guitars. Also, the shorter scale produces a warmer tone but lacks the crisp response and bell-like chime of the Fender. Which is better? Well, that's up to the player and there are many who prefer the PRS scale length, which splits the difference. Any guitar can have reduced string tension and a warmer tone just by tuning it down, as Jimi Hendrix did with his Strat. Using heavy strings, like Stevie Ray Vaughan did, can make up for the reduced string tension on a down-tuned guitar. These and other options provide many possible avenues for tone geeks to explore on their endless quest for that magic combination of great tone and playability.

Acoustic Note: It's easy to imagine that the difference in playability between acoustic and electric guitars is entirely due to the lighter strings that electrics tend to be strung with. Electric guitars commonly come new from the factory strung with .009 light-gauge strings while acoustics come with .011s. This makes a big difference, but so does the fact that acoustics usually have a slightly longer scale length. The chart below shows the scale lengths of a few electric guitars for reference and comparison.

Scale Length Guide

GUITAR	SCALE LENGTH
Fender Stratocaster	25.5"
Fender Telecaster	25.5"
PRS Custom 24	25"
PRS Custom 22	25"
Rickenbacker Model 330	24.75"
Gibson Les Paul Standard	24.75"
Gibson SG Standard	24.75"
Fender Jaguar	24"
Fender Mustang	22"

Frets

There are many things to consider about frets, the first and foremost being their height. After a few years of playing—the amount of time will vary from player to player—fret wires can become worn down and dinged. Intonation and playability can start to go downhill. These are signs your frets need maintenance work.

Fret Maintenance

When you play a guitar with new frets and notice passages that you have been having difficulty with are now suddenly easier, or chord voicings with questionable intonation on your guitar now ring true, then you should realize your guitar is overdue for a fret *leveling* and *dressing*. Leveling and dressing the frets is the process of filing and sanding the frets smooth so they perform like new, though they will be a little lower in height. Edging work may also be needed if the fingerboard has dried out and shrunken so that the frets stick out over the side. These procedures should be done by a trained professional. A guitar can usually handle five to ten levelings before requiring a complete re-fretting (completely replacing the frets). The taller and wider the frets, the more levelings they can withstand. If your guitar has gone too long between levelings, then a fewer number of levelings will be possible. Replacing the frets is a fairly expensive job, but it will really bring your instrument back to life.

Worn fret in need of leveling and dressing.

Fret Type and Size

The fret wire is attached to the fingerboard via a square metal tang which is hidden from view under the *crown,* or top, of the fret (see illustration below). The width and height of the crown are both important considerations. Since the fret location defines a note's exact pitch, the thinner the width of the crown the better the intonation. But, thinner frets will also wear out faster. Taller, wider frets are generally preferred by string benders and shredders, because they reduce resistance against the fingerboard to make it easier to play fast technical music. The drawback with tall, wide frets is too much finger pressure can cause the strings to go sharp. At first, this may seem like a major issue, but it might be best to learn to adapt from the higher pressure required to play a steel-string acoustic guitar, without buzzing, to the feathery light touch required for electric guitars with light strings and jumbo frets.

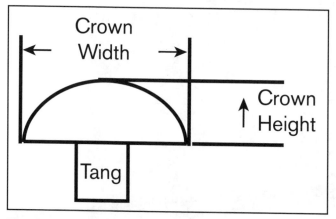

Illustration of fret.

Fret wires are made from a variety of metals, including nickel, soft nickel, brass, stainless steel, and nickel-free copper alloy. Each of these feature different hardnesses that will affect their durability and ease of maintenance for the luthier.

Number of Frets

Another important question to ask is how many frets do you need? Most electric guitars have 22, but the number of frets available on most standard models range from 21 to 24. Of course it's a matter of personal choice, but if your style of playing demands bending the D note at the 22nd fret of the 1st string up to E, then you might want a 24-fret instrument. If you play a lot at the high end of the guitar neck, then you might even consider something like the Ibanez Xiphos guitar, which has 27 frets.

Photo by Tobias Hurwitz

27-fret Ibanez Xiphos.

Neck Profile

The shape of the guitar neck affects the feel of a guitar in a prominent and immediately noticeable way. It should really be a make-or-break factor when selecting a new guitar. Playability and tone are always things to consider, but easier playability usually results in a weaker tone. A fatter neck produces more sustain and a fatter tone, but it's harder to do things like wrap your thumb around the top of the neck like Jimi Hendrix, or stretch your fingers out really far like Eddie Van Halen. Technical players tend to prefer thinner necks with the "D" shape pictured below.

If you happen to own a few guitars, check to see if you can identify the neck profile of each and re-evaluate what you like and dislike about the feel and tone of each guitar. Next time you're in a music store, see if you can find a neck profile that feels really great. How's the tone? Can you fatten it up by tweaking the amp, or do you really just need a fatter neck? Most of us will go for playability, because if it doesn't feel good, then you're not likely to sound good either way.

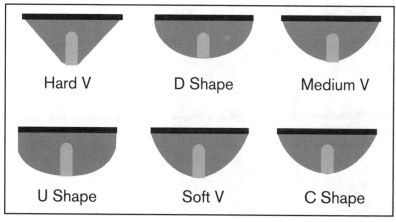

Neck profile chart.

Tuning Pegs (Machine Heads)

Tuning pegs, or machine heads, on a guitar come in many varieties—from the violin-style wooden pegs used on old-school Spanish guitars to the modern mechanical tuners that turn by themselves via computer control on the Gibson Robot Guitar. The two major types of tuning pegs are standard and locking.

Standard pegs all have one thing in common: the string is attached to the post by winding it. In the case of vintage-style Fender tuning pegs, the string end is fed down into a hole in the tuning peg post, which secures it nicely for wrapping. Most other tuners have a hole cut through the post for the string to pass through before wrapping.

Photo by Tobias Hurwitz

Vintage-style Fender tuner.

Standard Gibson-style tuner.

Locking tuners are mainly for use on guitars with whammy bars. Sperzel introduced locking tuners in 1983, and PRS popularized them in 1986. The idea behind locking tuners is the string locks directly onto the post with no wrapping needed, speeding up the stringing process and eliminating tuning problems. Many players choose to upgrade to locking tuners, whether or not a trem is installed.

Sperzel-style locking tuners made by Fender.

The Nut

The nut is situated at the end of the fingerboard, near the headstock. Its slots support and space the strings properly, holding them at the correct level so they don't buzz against the first few frets. If the nut is set too high, the guitar will have high action and poor intonation, while if it's set too low, there will be buzzing. Some nuts are made of metal, mostly on bass guitars, and feature screws that adjust the height of each string or the overall height of each side of the nut. This is a very useful feature for relieving fret buzz quickly and easily.

Height-adjustable nut on Warwick Thumb Bass.

Various materials have been used to construct the nut, including bone, wood, plastic, ivory, metal, and graphite. Plastics, graphite, and other non-slip materials are used on guitars with whammy bars to help alleviate tuning problems that result from strings getting stuck in the nut and not returning to their original positions after whammy use. This system, combined with a straight headstock and locking tuners, is used by Fender on its Deluxe American Stratocaster, PRS on its Custom 24, and by many other whammy-equipped guitars.

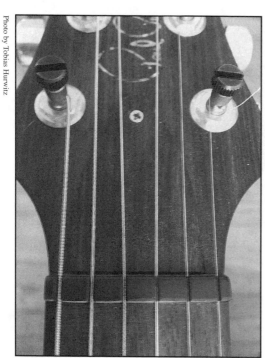

PRS Custom 24 with super slippery synthetic nut.

The Locking Nut

The locking nut is another option for staying in tune while using the whammy bar, and it is usually found in conjunction with a Floyd Rose double-locking tremolo. The locking nut tightens each string individually, so even if a string breaks, the tension will not change between the nut and the tuner. Locking nuts do their job well but are somewhat inconvenient when it comes to changing strings and tuning (as we discovered earlier in this book), since an Allen wrench is required to make adjustments.

Photo by Timothy Phelps

Ibanez JS Series with locking nut.

Roller nuts offer yet another solution to whammy-induced tuning problems.

Photo by Tobias Hurwitz

Roller nuts.

The signature Gibson Johnny A. model is equipped with a standard nut. Johnny himself lubricates the nut so that he can use a traditional Bigsby tremolo much more actively than one might expect and still stay in perfect tune. We'll cover the Bigsby tremolo on page 210.

Photo by Patrick Keenan, The Twelfth Fret, Inc.

Signature Gibson Johnny A. guitar.

The Compensated Nut

A *compensated nut* is designed to eliminate or improve tuning problems inherent with the guitar. A piano also has inherent tuning problems, but tempering helps spread the tuning issues out evenly over the range of the instrument, making them mostly unnoticeable. The compensated nut attempts to solve this problem. It features string notches in the nut that are cut slightly differently to allow for individual string length to be slightly shortened or lengthened according to the best judgment of a luthier or designer. This system certainly improves intonation and is especially popular on acoustic guitars whose bridges don't tend to be adjustable.

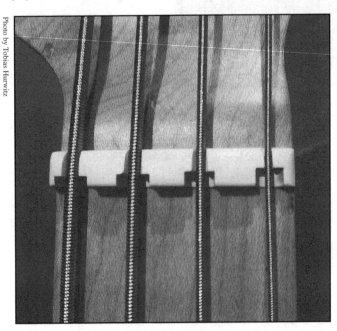

Compensated nut.

This is a custom compensated nut, which adjusts the ratio of the scale length versus the fretted length of each string. This allows "in tune" playing both at the lower open chords as well as the entire neck.

The Bridge

Guitar strings make first contact with the body of the guitar at the bridge. The strings may be attached to the bridge or to a tailpiece located next to the bridge. Bridge styles include the simple, wooden Danelectro bridge; the fully adjustable, whammy-equipped Floyd Rose; and the ultramodern, automatically self-tuning EverTune bridge.

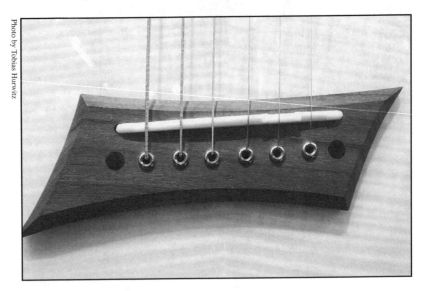

Photo by Tobias Hurwitz

Simple bridge on Michael Kelly electric archtop.

The more adjustable a bridge is, the more control the guitarist will have over action and intonation. The Gibson Tune-o-matic is a good example of a highly adjustable bridge. It features individual string saddles that are adjustable up, down, forward, and backwards, and the overall bridge height is adjustable with two sturdy screws on each side.

The bridge must be properly set for a guitar to have good action and intonation. In some cases, there are fine tuners conveniently located on the bridge so that tuning can be done with the picking hand during performances.

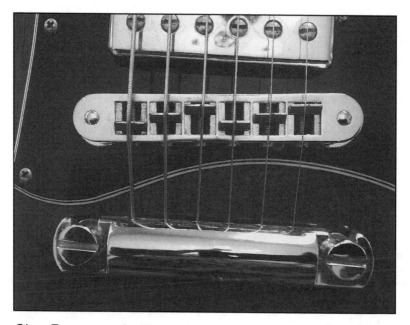

Gibson Tune-o-matic bridge.

One of the most notable modern innovations in bridge design is the EverTune bridge. This mechanical wonder maintains perfect tension and tuning for each string with an ingenious series of springs and levers concealed in the guitar's body. The EverTune system requires special routing for installation, and thin-bodied guitars, such as the Gibson SG, are not compatible with the system. The device keeps your guitar in perfect tune for the life of the strings, even with string bending!

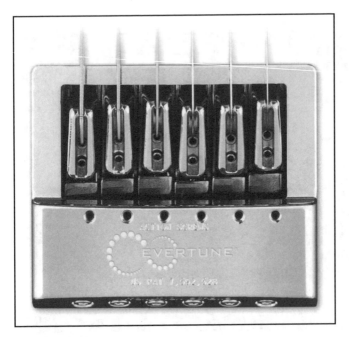

EverTune bridge.

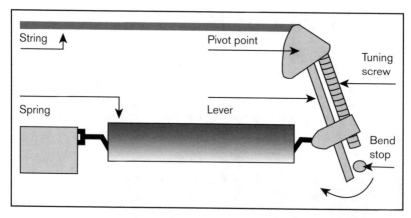

The mechanics behind the EverTune bridge.

The Whammy Bar

The whammy bar (also known as the tremolo bar, as we learned on page 100), raises or lowers the pitches of the strings, enabling a wide range of effects from gentle chord vibrato to full dive bombs, chirping sounds, siren wails, and more. The old-school Bigsby-style units mount to the top of the guitar without physical alterations, such as routing. Bigsbys are mainly used for gentle vibrato and slight dipping of the strings for which they function beautifully.

Bigsby whammy bar.

The vintage Strat-style whammy bar is capable of many wonders in the hands of the likes of Jimi Hendrix, but it wreaks havoc on tuning and is plagued with other problems. For instance, the threaded bar itself requires being screwed farther and farther in each time so that it becomes rare, if not impossible, to position in a consistently comfortable position. Vintage guitar purists still swear by these whammy bars, but those of us who simply want to play in comfort and with good intonation tend to choose more modern alternatives.

Vintage Fender whammy bar.

In addition to the Floyd Rose system, which we have already discussed in depth (pages 99–145), there is the Paul Reed Smith–style floating trem. Like the Floyd Rose, the PRS bar doesn't thread in, so it conveniently stays where you want it and maintains tuning very well. Strings don't slip at the bridge on the PRS trem, and the headstock and nut are designed to eliminate slippage at the other end—achieved through the use of locking tuners, a slippery nut, and a straight string pull to the pegs.

On the next page, we'll look at how to lock down, or "block," a tremolo.

Locking Down a Trem (Blocking)

Many players have guitars with whammy bars they don't ever use. If the bar is *floating*, you'll encounter tuning problems when you break a string, and the pitches of other strings will change when you play harmonized bends—not to mention the hassle of having to constantly loosen and tighten the locking nut.

The tremolo system features a rectangular metal block that extends down into the guitar's body with springs attached to it. In a floating setup, the block can move a short distance in either direction before resting against the edge of the cavity of the guitar body. A block of wood or material such as cork or cardboard can be fitted into the spaces around the metal block to immobilize it. This keeps the bridge in one position and deactivates the whammy bar. This is called *blocking* the trem. If you don't use the bar, the best thing to do is block, or lock down, the trem. After blocking the trem, you can remove the whammy bar itself, the springs, and the locking parts of the nut, and the guitar will function more efficiently. It is very easy to unblock a trem to return the guitar to its original condition.

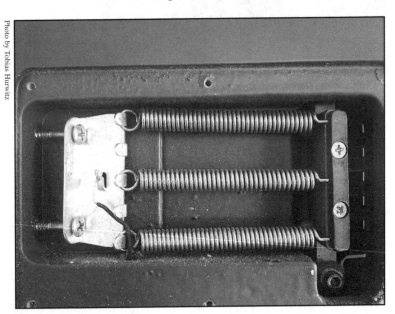

Photo by Tobias Hurwitz

Unblocked floating trem.

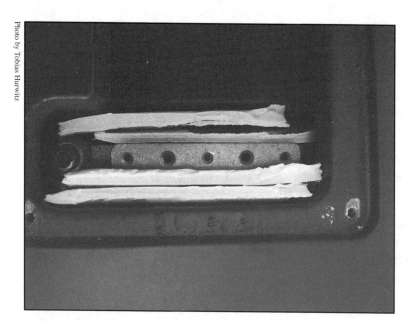

Blocked floating trem.

Understanding Guitar Amps

An amplifier is much more than just a device that makes your guitar louder. Many consider it a musical instrument unto itself and rightly so. Guitar amps are divided into two main categories: *tube* and *solid state*. Tube amps use old-school vacuum tubes to amplify the signal, whereas solid-state amps use modern transistors. The controversy regarding the superiority of tubes over solid state, and of course digital emulation, continues to rage even after decades of research and development in these areas. Tube amps have created a huge palette of wonderfully warm and dynamic tones that are etched into our memories from decades of exposure. Tube amp sounds have been everywhere—from the jazz of Charlie Christian and the blues of B. B. King to the surf music of The Ventures and the classic rock of bands like The Beatles, The Rolling Stones, Pink Floyd, and Led Zeppelin.

Tube Amps

As a tube amp is played louder, its power tubes work harder and the result is the pleasing but elusive sound known as *power tube distortion*. Tubes are also very sensitive to playing touch (dynamic range), so it's possible to clean up a gritty sound just by playing softer. And, conversely, a player may dig in a bit harder with the pick to make the amp really growl. These two factors, power tube distortion and touch sensitivity, are the main talking points of those who champion tubes over solid state.

Solid-State Amps

Early transistorized solid-state amps didn't sound nearly as good as tube amps. They were flat, sterile, and somewhat "cold" in comparison to tube amps. Yet, the lightweight, cheap, and dependable transistor was too great a temptation for manufacturers to resist. The potential was there, and it obviously just needed some tweaking. After a lengthy period of development, the microchip joined forces with the transistor to spawn the premium solid-state and tube amps of the modern era. Newer solid-state amps incorporate digital modeling technology to closely copy the sounds of classic tube amps, speaker cabinets, stomp boxes, and more. Some of them even include an actual tube preamp, mostly as a marketing tool, but also to combine the two technologies for enhanced tone. Perhaps these new amps don't sound precisely identical to tube amps, but they are lighter, less expensive, more reliable, and sound great nonetheless.

Modern tube amps feature many improvements like multi-mode channels, MIDI switching, digital reverb, and variable wattage control. Tube amps, solid-state amps, and digital modeling amps are all available as combo amps, or as separate speakers and amp heads. We'll discuss these options next.

The Combo Amp

The *combo amp* combines the amplifier and speaker into one convenient package. Combo amps range in size from very small practice amps to large powerful ones ready for the stadium stage. They can be simple or heavily laden with features. The one pictured below is called a 2x12 because it's loaded with two 12" speakers. 1x12 and 1x10 configurations are also common.

Photo by Michael A. Walley of Sam Ash Music, Clearwater, FL.

The Vox AC30 2x12 combo pictured above was used by both John Lennon and George Harrison throughout their early work with The Beatles.

Amp Heads and Stacks

A half stack combines a separate amp head with a single 4x12 speaker cabinet. Separate amp heads often have more features than combos and can be easily matched with different speakers to achieve a variety of sounds. Amp heads are often paired with several cabinets to create full stacks, which can be seen chained together at stadium rock shows, or they may be matched with smaller cabs for studio sessions or small gigs.

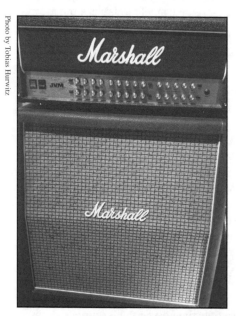

Marshall JVM 100-Watt Half Stack.

Fancy Modern Amps: *The Marshall JVM 100-watt half stack features four foot-switchable channels, each of which has three modes and individual digital reverb controls. It has two master volumes, which means any of its four channels can be individually boosted by hitting a foot switch, or all four can be turned up or down simultaneously with a rotary knob. The back panel features MIDI ports for integration with other devices, two effects loops (one is foot-switchable), and a compensated direct-out jack which enables pristine recording without the use of a speaker cabinet or microphone.*

Basic Amp Features

The average player may not need all the extra features found on a flagship Marshall or Mesa/Boogie amp. Amplifiers these days may have a lot of features, but when you shop for an amp there a few basic features to look for: channel switching, reverb, and an effects loop. *Channel switching* allows the user to switch (via a foot switch) between one channel that might be set for a clean rhythm sound and another channel that might be set for a louder, distorted lead sound. Channel switching makes the amp much more versatile when playing live. Basic two-channel models are the most common, but three- and four-channel amps are also available to offer even more versatility.

Reverb creates a soft, spacious sound that is essential to surf, country, jazz, rock, blues, and metal music. It's ideal for each channel of an amp to have its own reverb knob, since higher amounts of gain will dampen or suppress reverb.

The *effects loop* is a feature that players might not understand right away but will certainly appreciate when its full capacity becomes apparent. If you love the distortion tone on your amp's lead channel but also want to use delay, chorus, or another wet effect with it, then the effects loop is your solution. (Note: A wet effect is created by a signal that has been altered, or *modulated*. A *dry* signal is unaltered. For more on wet and dry effects, see Flow, page 227.) Effects pedals or devices can be patched into the loop, thereby inserting them post-distortion, which is the proper place for wet effects in the signal chain. Plugging directly into the effects return jack of the loop allows players who use floor-based multi-effect units to bypass the preamp section of the amp and use only the power amp section, thereby getting the best tone possible from their gear.

Boutique Amps

Boutique amplifiers became very popular in the 1990s and have since become a force to be reckoned with in the industry. These small batches of handmade tube amps are intended to be of a higher quality than what is available from major manufacturers. Boutique amps tend to feature a heavy-duty chassis, class-A operation, point-to-point wiring, high-end speakers, leather corners, custom colors, and low- or variable-wattage settings. Trainwreck, Matchless, Budda, Fuchs, and Bruno are some of the most popular boutique amp companies, and dozens more are emerging.

Point-to-Point Wiring

In the 1950s, the recently invented printed circuit board, or PCB, began replacing the labor-intensive point-to-point wiring methods that were the norm at the time. So, roughly, the first two decades of guitar amp production exclusively featured point-to-point wiring, and virtually everything else after was made with printed circuit boards. Today, boutique amp companies like Matchless offer small batches of handmade point-to-point tube amps. Occasionally, major companies like Fender or Marshall will produce a limited-edition run of point-to-point amps that faithfully reproduce the exact specs of a favorite vintage amp.

Many of the most desirable vintage amps contained printed circuit boards and their tones were actually better in some ways because point-to-point amps needed more shielding to avoid noise problems. Amps with point-to-point wiring are also harder to service because troubleshooting them is more difficult, and the repair will usually take longer due to its complex nature. On the up side, anyone offering a point-to-point amp today is doing so with the goal of making a better amplifier. These pricey little gems are likely to deliver cool and quirky features, great looks, great tones, and very fine craftsmanship. They are shielded carefully so if there is indeed an audible difference in the thicker gauge hand-soldered wiring, you'll be able to hear it. On the flip side, there are those among us who believe point-to-point amps are simply overpriced and overrated, and that the printed circuit board took over because it's cheaper and actually works better.

How to Chain Amps Together

When guitarists like Stevie Ray Vaughan use 10 or so amps at once, they're actually *chaining* them together. To chain amps together, plug your guitar into input 1 on the front panel of an amp, then use input 2 as an output to send the signal to the next amp. The process is then repeated to form a chain of amps. The same method was used by Jimi Hendrix to create his famed walls of Marshalls. The effects send or preamp output can also be used to drive additional amps. (For more on amps and effects loops, see the chapters on Understanding Speaker Cabinets, Ohmage and Impedance, Tubes, and Signal Flow and Level.)

Understanding Speaker Cabinets

Cabinets

The term *cabinet* refers to a separate enclosure that houses speakers. Guitar speaker cones are commonly available in 10", 12", and 15" sizes. Sizes smaller than 10" are usually reserved for combo amps. The term 4x12 means there are four 12" speakers in the cabinet; 2x10 indicates two 10" speakers, etc. Common speaker cabinet configurations are: 1x12, 2x12, 4x12, 4x10, and 1x15. Cabinets can be used as speakers for rack systems and as additional, auxiliary amplification for combo amps. They are mostly found as components in half stacks, full stacks, or larger amp systems.

Speaker Cones

Discriminating players demand high performance from their speakers. Some speaker cones add distortion, while others produce crystal-clear jazzy tones. The lower the wattage of a speaker, the more crunch (distortion) it will yield in high-volume situations. A Marshall 4x12 cabinet loaded with 25-watt Celestion speakers will distort much more quickly than the same cabinet loaded with 75-watt Celestions. If you prefer loud clean sounds, you will be best off with speakers made by a company that specializes in that area, such as Electro Voice. Most manufacturers offer a range of speaker options.

Open Back or Closed Back?

Fans of big, crunchy sounds usually prefer closed-back cabinets. The closed-back design causes sound waves to project with force from the front of the speaker. This helps create that chest-thumping quality of great rock and roll tone. Open-back cabinets allow sound waves to radiate from both sides, resulting in a more airy or ambient sound. This is typical of jazz, blues, and pop styles. Cabinets are available with removable panels for easy conversion. Companies like Budda and Mesa/Boogie also offer split cabinets, which are half open.

Open Back

*Rear view of a Peavey 1x12
extension cabinet with the panel
removed for open-back operation.*

Closed Back

*This Marshall 4x12 cabinet features a
closed back.*

Split Back

*Here is a rear view of a Budda 4x12 cabinet with a half-open back.
There are two more speakers in the lower, closed section.*

Ohmage and Impedance

The most important thing a guitarist should know in regard to *ohmage* is the way it affects how you connect a speaker cabinet or cabinets to an amp head. If you do it wrong, severe damage to the amp may occur. In fact, the amp may even catch on fire. Speakers are rated with ohmage values (e.g., 4 ohms, 8 ohms, 16 ohms, etc.) that reflect the electronic resistance of the speaker. Sometimes the speaker has several input jacks for selecting different ohmage loads and there may even be a toggle switch to select mono or stereo operation. To make matters more complicated, amps usually have three-way ohmage selector switches with settings for 4, 8, and 16 ohms. Some amps have multiple speaker outputs that are clearly labeled with various safe speaker combinations. Below are a couple of basic rules to follow.

Hooking Up One Speaker: This is very straightforward. Match the ohmage selector on the amp to the ohmage of the speaker, and plug it into the correct jack on the speaker. (The speaker may have more than one jack with different ohmages.)

Hooking Up Two Speakers: The ohmage selector must be set for half of the value of each speaker. For example: when hooking up two 16 ohm cabs, set the selector for 8 ohms. When connecting two 8 ohm cabinets, set the ohmage selector for 4 ohms, etc.

Tubes

Vacuum tubes, or valves, as they are called in England, have been a central component in guitar amp design since the dawn of the industry. Today, all amps either use tubes or attempt to imitate the sound tube amps have produced over the years.

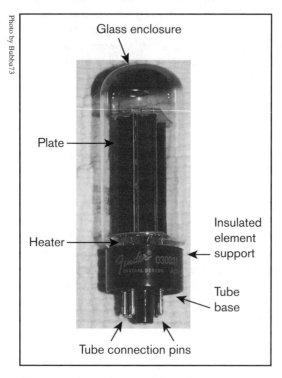

Vacuum tube with parts labeled.

Inside a Vacuum Tube

There are four main active electronic elements inside a vacuum tube: the plate, control grid, cathode, and heater (or filament, as it is sometimes called). The vacuum tube's glass enclosure creates a sealed-off environment in which these parts can heat up without burning. Preamp tubes essentially act as amplifiers that take the low voltage output of a guitar's pickup and transform it into a higher voltage signal that is strong enough to be processed by the preamp controls. The output tubes, which are also called the power tubes, then boost the signal even more, so it's strong enough to drive a speaker cabinet. The harder the tubes work, the hotter they glow and the faster they burn out.

There are three parts in an amp that commonly use tubes and they are: the preamp, power amp, and rectifier. (We'll discuss the rectifier on page 226.) Other circuits, such as the reverb unit or effects loop, may sometimes be driven or buffered by preamp tubes.

Preamp Tubes

The preamp section of a tube amp is the first thing a guitar signal passes through on its way to the speaker. Preamp tubes increase the wattage of the signal so it can then be processed by the preamp controls, which typically include gain, bass, midrange, and treble. The preamp stage is where distortion is primarily generated, and it may require several preamp tubes to achieve enough distortion—it all depends on the amp and the amount of gain desired. Preamp tubes do not need to be matched or *biased* (a concept we'll cover on page 226), so they can be replaced like light bulbs. The most common type of preamp tube for guitar amps is the 12AX7.

Power Amp Tubes

Guitar power amps commonly come in two types, *class A* and *class B*. Class-A amps operate with only one power tube and therefore have a lower wattage output than class-B amps. Class-B amps require a matched pair of at least two power tubes. The "push-pull" circuit at the heart of this design requires equal numbers of matched tubes on either side, so it will run on two, or four tubes, depending on the power output requirements. Class-A amps are free of the distortion that is an artifact of the push-pull design of class-B amps. In a nutshell, class-A amps create lower power, but more pure sound. Class-B amps are common and create the higher wattage levels that most people use. The EL34 and 6L6 are the most common types of power tubes for guitar amps.

Biasing

Unlike preamp tubes, power tubes cannot be changed easily. Power tubes must be biased by a qualified technician so that the power level of each tube is properly matched. The cost of maintenance that needs to be done regularly is one of the drawbacks of tube amps. How often you change your power tubes will depend on the hours and intensity of your use. With common use, expect to re-tube or re-bias roughly once a year, with a cost of about a few hundred dollars. There's some relief with Mesa/Boogie amps, which feature self-biasing circuits on some models that allow you to switch out matched sets of power tubes without re-biasing. For example, if you'd like to try 6L6 power tubes, which sound more like Fender amps than EL34s which deliver Marshall tone, you can select the tube type with a toggle switch and install them without any biasing. The other tubes in a guitar amp, the preamp and rectifier tubes (which we'll cover below), can be changed without biasing.

Note: *Tube amps are high-voltage devices that can electrocute you, so servicing should be done by qualified technicians. If you're switching a tube at home, turn the amp off and unplug it from the wall just to be safe. Oh, and make sure you're using the correct tube!*

Rectifiers and Rectifier Tubes

A guitar signal never passes through the *rectifier* circuit of an amp. The rectifier is a device that "rectifies," or corrects, electrical current for the high-voltage power supply, basically converting AC voltage into DC voltage. The only effect a tube rectifier has on your tone is a subtle sonic byproduct of a "sag" in the consistency of the power. This is a result of the inefficiency of a tube rectifier; a solid-state rectifier will produce better results. Some players like the sound of a tube rectifier, however, so Mesa/Boogie introduced a line of amps that give the user the option to switch between tube and solid-state rectifiers.

Signal Flow and Level

The terms *signal flow* and *signal level* refer to the order in which devices are situated in a signal chain (flow), and the amount of input and output signal sent to and from various devices (level). Putting your effects in the correct order and making sure each one is sending and receiving the right amount of signal is absolutely essential to properly configuring your rig and getting the best tones possible.

Flow

The order in which effects are placed in the signal chain greatly affects their sound, but there are no unbreakable rules. An important tip to remember, though, is gain-changing effects should come before wet effects in the signal chain. Gain-changing effects include: fuzz, overdrive, distortion, phase shifter, clean boost, EQ, compressor, wah, auto-wah, noise gate, and envelope filter (or follower). The exception is the volume pedal, which is usually placed last in line. Wet effects include: reverb, delay, chorus, flanger, harmonizer, and the whammy pedal.

An example of a tried-and-true signal chain is the following:

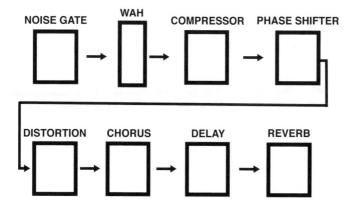

Tip: *Phase shifters, flangers, and the whammy pedal may be freely moved around the signal chain without worry. They sound good anywhere, but their location before or after distortion will sound quite different. Their placement is up to the user.*

Try effects in different configurations to see what you like. Sometimes a "mistake" can produce a happy accident. Try hooking up a wah pedal backwards, and you'll get the cool sound that David Gilmour stumbled upon for the song "Echoes" from *Meddle*. Gilmour discovered an effect that sounds like seagulls!

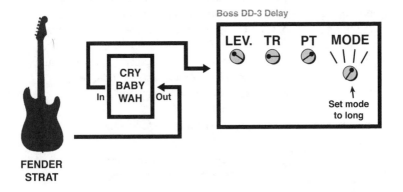

Guitar Gear Levels

There are several kinds of signal level for guitar gear.

1. **Consumer line level:** The *nominal* level, or level in which a device is designed to operate, for consumer audio is -10dBV, which means minus 10 decibels. In other words, it's very soft and perhaps a bit noisy. Consumer line level is used to transmit audio signals from CD players to amps and from one stomp box to the next.

2. **Professional line level:** The nominal level for professional audio is +4dBu, which basically means a lot louder with less background noise. Professional line level is used in rack-mounted units and other high-end gear.

High-end guitar equipment will usually include a button labeled -10/+4 near the input jack or effects loop. This must be set properly to accommodate the incoming signal, matching the gear being plugged in. If it isn't set correctly, the sound will be either very weak and distant or way too loud and unpleasantly distorted. Professional-grade gear will sometimes include input level meters or LED overload lights. Green is used to indicate healthy signal flow, and red means too much signal. Depending on the *headroom* (see definition below) of a given device, optimal levels will usually flash red once every second or so without staying all the way in the red, which is called *pegging*. A good signal is robust enough to drive the device without being so high that it distorts its input stage. Your ear will become accustomed to identifying level mismatches over time. When it sounds right, then the levels must have been set right. If expensive gear sounds horrible, check the levels!

About headroom: *Headroom is the amount of gain above nominal level (0 VU) that a device can receive before clipping. Lots of headroom is good for rack mounted delay units and similar devices whose aim is to affect a guitar's signal without adding distortion. Lower headroom on, say, the input of a guitar amp is also good because it allows the player to easily overdrive the amp with a boost pedal or high-output pickup.*

More About Effects Loops

We have previously mentioned that wet effects should come post-distortion in the signal chain. This might pose a problem if, for example, you like the distortion that comes from your amp's heavy channel but would like also to be able to use your favorite delay pedal for some sweet echo. Enter the effects loop. The effects loop inserts a signal after the preamp, which produces the distortion, but before the power amp, which amplifies the overall sound. Therefore, all wet effects should be run in the loop if amp distortion is to be used. They can also be added post-amplifier through a mixing desk during a live performance or recording session. The send of the loop goes to the input of the wet effect, and the return of the loop is connected to the output of the wet effect.

Trick of the trade: *If you wish to bypass the preamp section of a guitar amp and only use it as a power amp, then plug your guitar directly into the effects return jack. Players who use multi-effect units should not plug them straight into the front of an amp. Multi-effects units usually include preamps, and it's not ideal to run one preamp into another.*

Noise

If there's one thing electric guitarists actually agree on, it's that noise is bad and the less of it in your guitar sound the better.

Let's first learn about the terms used to describe noise. There is always a small amount of noise inherent in most audio signals. This is called the *noise floor*. Think of when you plug a guitar with a single-coil pickup into a loud amp and don't play anything but still hear some noise. That is the noise floor. Now if you strum a chord, chances are you won't notice the noise while the chord is ringing, because the chord is so much louder than the noise. The chord is called the *signal*. The difference between the volume of the chord and the volume of the noise is called *signal-to-noise ratio*. As the chord fades, the noise becomes more apparent and there will be a point where the chord becomes lower in volume than the noise. This is the *threshold*. Most of us simply turn the volume knob down on our guitar when a note or chord fades away. This silences the noise at the threshold point. There is a device that does this automatically, and it is called a *noise gate*. A noise gate is the most popular way to deal with noise, and it usually functions best when placed first in the signal chain. That way, it works just like turning the volume knob down on your guitar.

- *Sensitivity* (sens) sets the threshold at which the gate closes.

- *Decay* controls the speed of the gate closing.

Boss Noise Gate NF-1 pedal.

Noise Reduction

Gadgets like the Rocktron Pro Hush II are called *noise reduction* units. They combine frequency-specific gating technology with downward expansion technology and work even better than simple noise gates. Noise reduction units actually improve the signal-to-noise ratio instead of merely silencing the noise before the signal starts and after it fades (as a noise gate would do). Units like the Pro Hush II function best in the effects loop of an amp or somewhere in the effects chain after which the noise has been introduced in the signal. If you're running an old-school rack system with many units chained together and simultaneously responding to the commands of a MIDI foot controller, this is the way to go. Noise reduction units work quite splendidly and can be bypassed or set to handle anything from slight noise to heavy noise.

Noise Is Everywhere

Noise can come from many sources. It could come from gain-altering devices, like compressors or distortion pedals, or from a bad tube in your amp. Noisy single-coil pickups, inadequate shielding inside the body cavity of your guitar, or too many tangled wires and wall-wart power adapters contribute to noise problems. Noise can come from your rig being close to appliances like light fixtures. The electricity which powers your rig can be "dirty" due to the ground wire picking up noise. Noise is everywhere and results from a combination of many different factors.

Scrubbing the Noise

Noise can also be removed from a recorded track by *scrubbing* the track. The sections of noise floor that are recorded before the guitar starts playing and all the little gaps of noise between notes can be deleted by an audio engineer through editing. The engineer would cross-fade the beginning and end of some or all of the notes to make the editing sound natural. When reverb is applied to the track after scrubbing, it fills each gap with depth, helping to glue it all together into a perfectly natural sound.

Furman Power Conditioner (see page 234 for an explanation of power conditioners).

Ebtech Hum Eliminator.

Rocktron's HUSH Pedal.

Other Ways to Reduce Noise in Your Rig

If possible, it's best to build a rig that avoids the need for noise gates or noise reduction. These units are costly, take up valuable space on a pedalboard or in a rack system, and must be set correctly to avoid unpleasant side effects. In the case of the noise gate, the tail end of sustained notes may flutter or be abruptly cut off. Noise reduction can dull the overall tone and also shorten sustain if used too much, so it's best to use these devices only when there is no alternative. Let's break down other ways to reduce noise in your rig.

Power: All grounded appliances in most buildings are essentially connected through the ground wire, which is the third wire—the one with the longest prong in a three-prong plug. Any noise-causing interference generated by such appliances is called "dirt." Use a quality power conditioner to eliminate dirt in the power. High-end power conditioners have digital voltage readouts, so you can tell if the power is weak or in flux. If the power is too high, the conditioner will limit voltage to 110. If it's too low, the power will be boosted by battery backup to the desired 110 volts. Power conditioners will help your rig run noise-free. Also, check for a ground lift switch on your amp, processor, or power supply. It can eliminate the *60 cycle hum* caused by ground loops. The 60-cycle hum and other noise problems may also be eliminated by power conditioning.

Note: *The United States uses a 110 volt/60 hertz standard power system, while Europe uses a 220volt/50 hertz system. Some American made guitar gear comes equipped to work with the European system, but most does not.*

Cabling: Shorter cables and cables with heavier gauges will produce less noise, so always try to use the best quality cable you can afford at the shortest possible length that you'll need.

Single-coil pickups: If you're playing a vintage Strat-style guitar with a five-position blade switch, there will be single-coil hum in pickup positions 1, 3, and 5. Remember, positions 2 and 4 combine adjacent pickups for a "humbucking" sound that kills the noise. Noiseless single-coil pickups now come standard on many Stratocasters and are available as replacement pickups. They are dead quiet and sound great!

Shielding: The electronics cavity in your electric guitar is supposed to be covered with shielding that has been painted on, foil taped, or both. If it isn't properly done, there will be noise problems. Have a skilled technician look over your guitar to make sure it's properly shielded.

Too much gain from combining the wrong effects: Running two distortion pedals together or combining a compressor and a distortion pedal will likely cause a lot of noise. Running a hot signal from an active pickup can also throw off the gain balance in your rig and make everything sound noisy. You may have to work with less distortion and sustain to enjoy a low-noise system.

Tubes: Tubes wear out eventually and sometimes become *microphonic*. A tube that is microphonic can produce noise or feedback. Tapping on your tubes gently, while the amp is on, will reveal a bad tube if you have one. When you tap on a bad tube, it will make a ringing sound. If the offending tube is a preamp tube, you can replace it without re-biasing or retubing the whole amp. If it's a power tube, you'll need to replace all of the power tubes and possibly re-bias the amp. Obviously, tubes are hot and operate at high voltage. So be very careful, or just have an authorized technician deal with your tubes.

Take notice of these preventative measures, and you may never need a noise gate or reducer.

Physical and Virtual Effects

Knowing about physical effects will be tremendously useful when you have to program their counterparts in the virtual world. Physical effects exist in every form—from stomp boxes and tape echoes to rack-mounted units and everything in between. Play with the knobs on stomp boxes and get to know the wiring of amps, mics, and pedalboards. The experience gained will help you better understand virtual effects when you encounter them in plug-ins and software.

Since the names of the actual effects units are trademarked, companies like Line 6 and Roland use clever monikers to refer to the gear they are emulating. For instance, a "Script Phaser" is a clone of a vintage MXR Phase 90 that features the script logo. A "Modern California" amp refers to a Mesa/Boogie Mark IV or similar amp.

Below, we have illustrated a simple signal chain on a pedalboard.

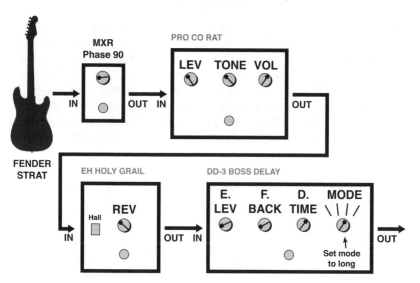

Below is the same signal chain as above but displayed on the "grid" page of the Axe-Edit software provided by Fractal Audio Systems for their Axe-FX II processor. When you click on an individual pedal in the software, its controls are accessed via a drop-down screen. Note how the virtual compressor has the same three knobs as the real one.

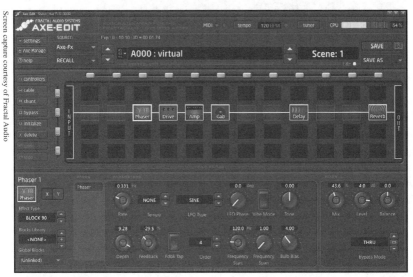

Axe-FX II screen.

The AmpliTube app for the iPhone or iPad can create the same signal chain that we've been studying. See below.

AmpliTube app for the iPod or iPad.

This signal chain, or any other, can be easily created in various digital environments. But do the digital models stack up to the real thing? It will be up to you to decide which sounds more authentic. After you compare for authenticity, you should probably decide which actually sounds better. At some point, technology must evolve beyond tubes and tangled wires. Do you really want to hear the hum of questionable power supplies and aging wires, lug all of that stuff around, and fix it as it constantly breaks? Companies specializing in digital products, like Apple, Roland, Line 6, and Fractal Audio, would like to have you believe that the time has finally come to retire your tube amps, cabs, mics, and pedals. This continues to be a controversial issue. Only time will tell if the tube amp will go the way of the VCR or 8-track player.

Cabling

There are three types of cables that will fit into the output jack of your electric guitar, but only the ¼" shielded *instrument cable* is the correct choice. Shielded ¼" instrument cables are used to plug guitars into amps and pedals into each other. They have one ring on the male tip and usually say "instrument cable" on the side.

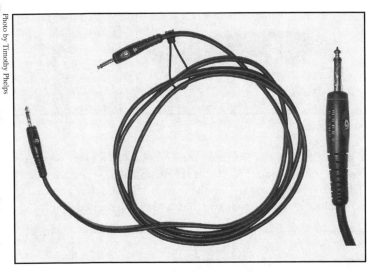

¼" instrument cable.

Don't confuse a *speaker cable* with the instrument cable. Speaker cables have one ring on the male tip, and they usually say "speaker cable" on the side. Some speaker cables feature two cables molded together like a small extension cord. Speaker cables should only be used to connect the output of an amplifier to the input of a speaker.

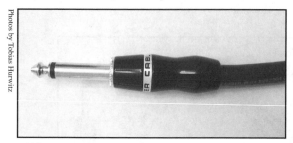

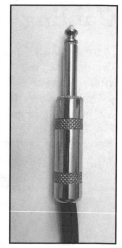

¼" speaker cables.

The third type of cable is the *TRS cable*, sometimes called a balanced stereo cable. (The "T" stands for tip, "R" stands for ring, and "S" represents sleeve.) TRS cables have two rings on the male ¼" tip, and they are used to connect expression pedals, foot switches, and rack-mounted gear.

TRS cable.

Instrument, speaker, and TRS cables all fit into the same ¼" jacks and carry at least some signal—even when being used for the wrong purpose. When the wrong cable is used, it can result in damage to amplifiers, and a weak, noisy tone.

Conclusion

A ton of information has been covered in this book. Now, you should feel comfortable maintaining your guitar and using a wide variety of equipment. Enjoy!